WISCONSIN
Field to Fork

FARM-FRESH RECIPES
from the
DAIRY STATE

LORI FREDRICH

Globe
Pequot

Essex, Connecticut

Globe Pequot

An imprint of Globe Pequot, the trade division of
The Rowman & Littlefield Publishing Group, Inc.
4501 Forbes Blvd., Ste. 200
Lanham, MD 20706
www.rowman.com

Distributed by NATIONAL BOOK NETWORK

British Library Cataloguing in Publication Information available

Library of Congress Cataloging-in-Publication Data
Names: Fredrich, Lori, author.
Title: Wisconsin field to fork : farm-fresh recipes from the dairy state /
   Lori Fredrich.
Description: Essex, Connecticut : Globe Pequot, [2023] | Includes index. |
   Summary: "This book aims to tell the tale of Wisconsin agriculture, not
   only through stories about the farmers who provide the wealth of
   vegetables, dairy, and livestock needed to sustain local restaurants but
   also through the recipes that take those products and weave magic into
   them"— Provided by publisher.
Identifiers: LCCN 2022056728 (print) | LCCN 2022056729 (ebook) | ISBN
   9781493067695 (cloth) | ISBN 9781493067701 (epub)
Subjects: LCSH: Cooking—Wisconsin. | Cooking (Natural foods)—Wisconsin. |
   Family farms—Wisconsin. | Farm produce—Wisconsin. | Cookbooks. lcgft
Classification: LCC TX907.3.W6 F74 2023 (print) | LCC TX907.3.W6 (ebook)
   | DDC 641.59775—dc23/eng/20221202
LC record available at https://lccn.loc.gov/2022056728
LC ebook record available at https://lccn.loc.gov/2022056729

∞™ The paper used in this publication meets the minimum requirements of American National Standard for Information Sciences—Permanence of Paper for Printed Library Materials, ANSI/NISO Z39.48–1992.

CONTENTS

FOREWORD: A CHEF'S PERSPECTIVE

As a young girl growing up in Southern California, I remember going to Plowboys Market to buy produce with my mom. We'd enter the market through these huge, gray roll-up doors and behind them we'd find a beautiful kaleidoscope of colors: fruits and vegetables in every shape and size, always local and always seasonal. It was my favorite of our weekly shopping stops. The watermelon, cantaloupe, and strawberries were so fragrant that you could smell them in the parking lot. I would walk around pointing at all the things I wanted my mom to buy. Of course, she'd patiently explain to me that we couldn't have everything. Sometimes she'd point out that a particular fruit or vegetable wasn't quite at its best yet. Often, she'd remind me that we simply couldn't consume everything I wanted to bring home.

We always think that the big moments are what will shape our lives. But I think that experience—which I can still visualize so clearly today—was my first step in understanding the importance of eating locally and seasonally.

When I moved to Wisconsin in 1995, I was so excited to experience the Midwest, as I had spent my entire life up to that point in California. When I began working in restaurants, I noted that every kitchen where I worked bought something from local farmers. But it was never a large amount. Part of the difficulty was that chefs had to put in the effort to connect with farms, develop relationships, and then arrange for pickup. Chefs always had the option to go to the farmers market, but at the time there weren't great options to get farm-fresh produce delivered to restaurants.

When I started at Barossa in 2004, the goal was to focus on Wisconsin-grown ingredients. We had a few small farms that we dealt with: Yuppie Hill Poultry, Growing Power, and Pin Oak Farms. This band of farmers helped me navigate this new landscape.

Early on, I took a tour of Growing Power's urban farm with the founder, Will Allen. At the time, their production was still small and we were purchasing lettuce, spinach, and a few other things from them. I still remember how much Will impressed me with his passion and desire to feed people fresh, delicious, healthy food. When I walked out of there that day, I knew I was committed to cooking with a new focus.

I started working more closely with Growing Power. Each season, they would come to us and ask what we were using, and they would plant vegetables to meet our needs. It was so inspiring for me, as a chef, to know that the spinach and salad mix that I was using had been picked early that morning.

My years in Milwaukee introduced me to the joy of seasonal cooking and the pleasure that each new season brought. But what really hit home for me was the flavor of the food I was using.

I remember the first time I purchased locally grown russet potatoes. I remember seeing this knobby, dirty little brown potato, scrubbing it clean and thinking, "I don't know about this." And then I tasted it. That little potato tasted like no other potato I had ever eaten. It was so full of flavor that I can only describe it as tasting of terroir.

These farmers were bringing me foods that I had used throughout my career. But the flavor surpassed anything I'd tasted before, and it made me see everything in an entirely new light.

By the time I opened my own restaurant, Meritage, I had amassed a growing list of local farmers with whom I worked. More and more, these people who grew the produce, who raised the lamb, the bison, the pork, and the chickens, were helping me shape my menus with every delivery. When they'd stop by, we'd talk about their lives and the hardships inherent to their work. But they'd also share the joy they felt when someone appreciated the fruits of their labor. It made me strive to make them

proud of what I was doing with what they worked so hard to produce. Effectively, we all grew together, and it was such a thrilling time for me.

Chefs can get distracted by many things. There is a great deal that goes into running a restaurant or kitchen. But whenever that delivery would come—when Al Weyker would drop off my order of bison from Lakeview Buffalo Farm or Lynn Lein would bring me chickens from Yuppie Hill Poultry—those moments were all about the connections between people. They would bring me back to my purpose as a chef: to honor those ingredients, cook with honesty and integrity, and let the beauty of the ingredients tell the story of the season.

My time in Wisconsin shaped so much of my life, not only as a chef but also as a person. I hope that when you read the stories and peruse the recipes from the people in this book, you will gain a new appreciation for the food you eat.

I also hope you will go out to your local farmers market and chat with the people who tend the land with such loving care. In addition, when you go to your favorite restaurant, I hope that you will see the care and love all the cooks and chefs put into showcasing these amazing ingredients from the magical place we call Wisconsin.

—Chef Jan Kelly

CREDITS, CLOCKWISE FROM TOP LEFT: FARM HAPPY, PARKSIDE SCHOOL, JESS BURNS, SAMANTHA SANDRIN, JOHN WEPKING, WISCONSIN GRASS-FED BEEF COOPERATIVE

THE POWER OF LOCAL FOOD

It was a dark, cold, dreary day in March when I opened my freezer and took out a quart-size bag of flash-frozen raspberries I'd procured from Centgraf Farms the previous September. I hesitated. It was my last bag, but I had plans to take the edge off the still unseasonably wintery weekend by using them to infuse Campari to make raspberry spritzes.

Just opening that bag made me feel a bit better. But as I popped one of the swiftly thawing berries into my mouth, something remarkable happened. I closed my eyes. The sweetness hit my tongue first, followed by subtle floral notes and tangy undertones as the berry warmed. I was utterly transported. It was summer again and I was back at the farmers market, gathering ripe fruits and vegetables in anticipation of this very moment in time.

That's the power of local food.

I love perusing the farmers market early in the season when local asparagus and fresh hoop-house spinach make their rare-but-delicious debuts; their flavor is nothing (nothing!) like the bland imposters sold in supermarkets. I find myself counting the days to the first appearance of (actually sweet) pea pods, Thumbelina carrots, Fairytale eggplants, and eventually sweet corn. And it's sheer bliss when plump, fresh-off-the-vine heirloom slicing tomatoes come into season, begetting the best BLTs and caprese salads I'll enjoy all year.

But I've gleaned even more joy from chatting with the farmers. Building relationships with them has not only given me a deep appreciation for their work but also built my knowledge about food. Farmers have taught me to taste the differences found in the produce grown in various soils and microclimates throughout the state. They've taught me to appreciate the flavor of truly great broccoli (it in no manner resembles the weeks-old heads we buy all winter from California) and how to cook fresh sunchokes. They've proffered lessons in the expansive flavor profiles of garlic, antique apples, and Asian greens.

I've always been food curious, but farmers have encouraged that quality, prompting me to regularly seek out vegetable varieties I've never tried. Those same farmers have taught me that if I want truly delicious berries in February, I need to buy them by the case while they're in season and freeze or otherwise preserve them. They've taught me that it's worth every penny to purchase a bag of hearty winter squash in early November for $20 because they'll easily keep until March in my basement pantry.

We all owe much to these masters of the soil. They work incredibly hard and give so much. Much like chefs—who incorporate the magic of fresh produce into artful, flavor-filled plates—these farmers use their science brains, their brawn, and their intuition to bring us food that's truly worth eating.

I hope this book inspires you to seek out something new at the farmers market, to strike up a conversation with a farmer and allow them to guide you in trying something novel (or at least new to you).

I also hope you'll be inspired to tackle a few of the more challenging recipes in this book, to stretch your skills and delve headlong into a culinary adventure. At the very least, I hope you take inspiration from them and they motivate you to expand your palate and try something wild, wonderful, and new.

I assure you it will be worthwhile. Quality ingredients are difficult to screw up, which is part of the magic of local food. Fresh, seasonal produce, meats, and grains lend themselves to delicious meals, sometimes with very little effort.

Most of all, I hope this book inspires you to take a moment to step back and appreciate the bounty of your local food scene: its farmers, its chefs, and its food.

FARMERS AND CHEFS

Within the past two decades, much has changed in the world of food. Farm-to-table dining has become best practice in restaurants across the country. Farmers have diversified their crops to meet the needs of both creative chefs and increasingly adventurous home cooks. Consumers have an increasing interest in connecting with those who make and grow their food. Meanwhile, chefs have played a crucial role in bridging the gap between the field and the fork.

Although states with longer growing seasons tend to take the credit for their ability to heed the call for local food, Wisconsin has been at the forefront of the movement. A great deal of credit for that role goes to Wisconsin's agricultural prowess. According to data from the Wisconsin Department of Agriculture, Trade and Consumer Protection, the state is the number one producer of cranberries and the number one exporter of ginseng root, whey, and sweet corn.

PAUL WEYKER

Wisconsin is home to a plethora of cherry and apple orchards. Farms in the Dairy State also harvest potatoes from 68,500 acres of land, ranking the state third in potato production. The state is a national leader in organic agriculture, with data from the Center for Integrated Agricultural Systems at the University of Wisconsin–Madison reporting that Wisconsin ranks second in the nation for overall number of organic farms and number one for organic field crop farms, livestock and poultry farms, and organic hog and pig farms.

Probably least surprising, Wisconsin is the country's largest producer of cheese (and fourth largest in the world), with nearly twelve hundred licensed cheesemakers who produce more than six hundred types, styles, and varieties of cheese, nearly double that of any other state. The state is home to the only Master Cheesemaker program outside of Europe.

Despite the shortcomings of a relatively brief growing season, the chefs in Wisconsin have capitalized on Wisconsin's bounty, offering increasingly localized seasonal menus and extending the harvest through active preservation. They have also brought notoriety to a former Midwestern "flyover zone" by excelling in their crafts and garnering accolades from organizations including the James Beard Foundation. In 2023, fourteen Wisconsin chefs, restaurants, and restaurateurs were named as semifinalists for the James Beard Awards in six categories.

For all of these reasons, this book aims to tell the tale of Wisconsin agriculture, not only through stories about the farmers who provide the wealth of vegetables, dairy, and livestock needed to sustain local restaurants but also through the recipes of chefs who take those fresh, local products and weave magic into them.

KALEIDOSCOPE GARDENS

Bits and Bites

Recipes

Featured Farms

Amy's Acre

Caledonia, Wisconsin
amysacre.com

Farming ran in Amy Wallner's family. Although her parents didn't manage one themselves, they'd both grown up on dairy farms. Her mother was also an avid gardener and stay-at-home mom who would often cook her way through the *Moosewood Cookbook* multiple times over a single summer. Having been spoiled by the bounty of fresh food she'd eaten at home, Amy says the transition to the processed cafeteria fare at the University of Wisconsin–Madison during college became a driving force in the direction she took with her education.

While she was a student, she took a job working on the research farm on the west side of Madison. Not only did she find the work inspiring, but she also found mentorship in her boss, who gave her confidence that there was a place for a woman like her in the agricultural sphere.

Her passions led her to intern at Milwaukee's Growing Power (an organization that led a national charge in urban agriculture and aquaponics for nearly thirty years) before pursuing agriculture work on the West Coast and eventually returning to Wisconsin to manage a garden for the Genesee Lakes School District in Oconomowoc. The garden supplied enough produce to operate a community-supported agriculture program for the teachers, with the goal of producing enough to supplement the fare in the school's cafeteria.

But she found her niche when she took a job in Milwaukee as a food runner at the former c.1880. Chef Thomas Hauck took an interest in the produce she grew and began purchasing items like Paris Market carrots, Dragon carrots, cucumbers, and tomatoes to use at the restaurant.

In 2014, when a farmer in Caledonia offered her land to start her own farm, she happily accepted. At the same time, she accepted a position as volunteer coordinator and farm hand at the Hunger Task Force Farm; the position assisted her in making ends meet while she built her

business, Amy's Acre. By 2019, she was farming full-time at her current property.

For the first few years, she sold exclusively to restaurants and to the Braise Restaurant Supported Agriculture program started by Chef Dave Swanson. For three seasons, she partnered with Heather Haneline, selling produce at the farmers market under the moniker Fine Fettle Farm and picking up additional restaurant customers including Chef Gregory Leon of Amilinda. But when Haneline decided to start a family, Wallner bought her share of the business and changed the name back to Amy's Acre.

Today, Amy farms about one and a half acres of a twenty-acre tract of land in Caledonia, Wisconsin, using regenerative farming methods to steward its fertile soil. Her goal is to work with the land and alongside nature to preserve the ecosystem without synthetic inputs. More recently, she added laying hens as a form of land management; the chickens are rotated on pasture, giving them free range to feed on worms, insects, and

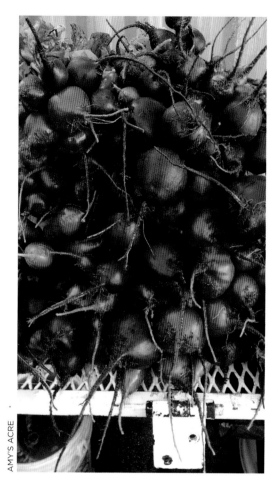

AMY'S ACRE

vegetation while giving back to the land in the form of fertilizer. Her farm focuses on open-pollinated heirloom vegetable varieties, including Purple Dragon carrots, heirloom tomatoes, and varieties of chicory and culinary herbs.

She sells her produce at local farmers markets, through a farm stand right on the property, and to select restaurants. Although restaurant sales no longer constitute the majority of her business, they remain a critical component of the business that reminds her of the farm's origin. Rather than cold-calling on restaurant accounts, Amy focuses on working with chefs she knows, or those who come to her via word of mouth, and she takes the time each season to sit down with them to debrief about the last growing season and plan for the next.

Amy says the joy of working with chefs is that not only do they value the power of fresh local food, but they also have the talents to turn her day-to-day products into dishes she would never have imagined. In addition, they share a similar lifestyle in which work is life and everything around it is intertwined.

Ultimately, farming is her calling. At its heart is the goal of nourishing others and connecting with humans who share her values in terms of the food they eat and the way it's produced. Farming is also a constant reminder that we are all connected to nature and even the littlest things can have a huge impact.

Beet Pate

Chef Gregory Leon, Amilinda
with beets from Amy's Acre

When you have lots of beets, why not make beet pate? This deep red pate is not only eye-catching but also sweet, earthy, and flavorful.

At Amilinda, they serve the pate spread on toasted sourdough bread with chopped tarragon, minced pickled shallots, and soft goat cheese. Feel free to substitute golden beets, which will give you a lovely pale yellow pate.

SERVES 10

2 teaspoons olive oil

2 pounds beets, roasted, peeled, and cut into 1-inch cubes

2 large shallots, thinly sliced

4 large garlic cloves or 2 large garlic scapes, thinly sliced

pinch of kosher salt and pepper

1 cup white wine

1½ cups cream

6 ounces goat cheese, room temperature

4 large eggs

4 large egg yolks

1 teaspoon salt

½ teaspoon black pepper

Preheat oven to 375°F.

In a large sauté pan, heat up the olive oil. Add the beets, shallots, and garlic or garlic scapes. Season with a pinch of salt and pepper and toss to combine. Add the wine and cook until the vegetables are soft and all the liquid has evaporated. Transfer to the jar of a blender.

Add the next six ingredients in order to the blender with the vegetable mixture and blend until completely smooth and combined. Pour the mixture into ten 4-ounce ramekins, and place the ramekins in a large baking dish. Fill the dish with hot water, enough to come halfway up the ramekins. Bake for 20 minutes.

Remove the pate from the oven to cool. Refrigerate for at least 45 minutes or until cold before serving.

LORI FREDRICH

Produce with Purpose

Fond du Lac, Wisconsin
producewithpurpose.com

Rick Slager's father was an avid gardener, so he grew up growing food. He recalls that the highlight of every year revolved around procuring seed catalogs and planning out the gardens for the season. But it wasn't until later in life, after spending much of his career running a lawn and landscaping business, that he found himself turning to farming as a second career. He describes the decision as "a bit of a midlife crisis."

He'd taken the opportunity to travel and work in West Africa for a year. While he was there, he dipped his toe into work with nonprofits in the agricultural sector. The experience was inspiring. But it also made him realize that, in order to make a difference, he needed to gain real-life experience in farming to adequately equip himself for the issues faced by farmers in more remote areas. So, in 2010, he founded Produce with Purpose, a farm born of his passion for food, his love for teaching people how to make use of farm-fresh produce, and his desire to make that food accessible to people from all walks of life.

Alongside his wife, Dawn, a veteran teacher who spent her summers working with him in the fields, he established two tillable acres of land, eventually renting additional acreage as needed. Their philosophy was simple: put more into the soil than you take out, and, in doing so, you'll create strong, healthy plants that can naturally fend off insects and disease. Along the way, he developed an affinity for storage vegetables, including carrots, specialty potatoes, beets, parsnips, and celery root.

For years, the couple farmed as many as twenty-one acres, selling produce to consumers through farmers markets as well as a traditional community-supported agriculture (CSA) program, which he upgraded to a build-your-own-box model in 2015 to stay ahead of the competition. They also built relationships with local chefs, many of whom became loyal, long-term customers. Rick credits his relationships with chefs with providing not only as much as 75 percent of his yearly income but also collegiality and a much-needed social outlet after spending his day "in the field with the crickets."

Things changed dramatically in 2020, as chefs were forced to pivot in response to the challenges of the COVID-19 pandemic. Restaurant business dwindled and staffing issues challenged farm operations. So Rick adjusted his business model, reducing his acreage and launching home delivery for customers in the Fox Valley and Green Bay areas. The move not only pulled his business through the pandemic but also gave him a robust new way to reach consumers with farm-fresh produce.

Rick, who began farming in his fifties and whose wife recently retired from teaching after thirty-four years, notes that his days working in the field are likely limited. However, he says his commitment to providing access to farm-fresh food is just beginning. Currently, he is working toward developing a food hub in the Fox Valley area that aims to streamline distribution for smaller farms located between Green Bay, Wisconsin, and Chicago, Illinois, making it easier for them to deliver their products to consumers, restaurants, and retailers.

PRODUCE WITH PURPOSE

PRODUCE WITH PURPOSE

Carrot Queso

Chef Mia Le Tendre, Strangetown
with vegetables from Produce with Purpose

This is Chef Mia Le Tendre's favorite vegan cheese sauce. It's both nut and soy free, which is rare for a vegan cheese dish. It's also less rich than the more common cashew cheeses and has a lower fat content. The starches from the russet potatoes work perfectly to mimic the gooey texture of traditional nacho cheese. When she hosts parties and gatherings at her home, she keeps a mini slow cooker of this sauce on her countertop with a bowl of tortilla chips. It's a crowd pleaser, even among her cheese-loving friends.

When she makes this dish at Strangetown, Mia uses carrots, potatoes, and onions from Produce with Purpose, a farm known for its high-quality root vegetables. For making at home, she recommends using russet potatoes for the best texture and bright orange carrots for the most aesthetically pleasing color.

MAKES 4 CUPS

12 cups water

2 large russet potatoes, peeled and cubed

2 orange carrots, peels on, cut into 1-inch rounds

¼ cup plus 2 tablespoons grapeseed oil, or other neutral oil, divided

¼ cup nutritional yeast

2 teaspoons distilled white vinegar

1 teaspoon sea salt

¾ cup water

½ cup red onion, fine diced

½ cup poblano pepper, fine diced

1 garlic clove, minced

1 teaspoon cumin

1 teaspoon smoked paprika

In a medium-size saucepan, bring 12 cups of water to a boil. Add potatoes and carrots. Boil for 8–12 minutes, until both potatoes and carrots are tender. Drain. Blend cooked vegetables, ¼ cup oil, nutritional yeast, vinegar, salt, and water in a high-speed blender, scraping the sides as needed. If you don't have a high-speed blender, you can use a food processor, but the result will not be nearly as smooth. Set blended mixture aside.

In a heated skillet, sauté onion and poblano in 2 tablespoons of oil until soft. Add garlic, and sauté another 1–2 minutes until fragrant and everything begins to brown. Add cumin and paprika, and cook for another minute. Remove from the heat and add the onion-poblano mixture to the blended carrot-potato mixture. Stir to incorporate. Taste for salt and adjust seasoning as needed. Serve with tortilla chips.

Centgraf Farms

Mayville, Wisconsin
centgraffarms.com

Resilient is among many words one could use to describe Centgraf Farms, a family-operated produce farm that dates back to 1926. It's a farm that wouldn't have survived had it not been for the family's dedication, hard work, and tenacity.

The farm was founded by Heinrich (Henry) and Katerina Centgraf, who immigrated to Wisconsin from Hungary in the 1890s. Henry, a master carpenter, dreamed of owning his own farm, so he saved money to purchase land by taking on jobs building scaffolding for a variety of prominent buildings cropping up in the burgeoning city of Milwaukee. Those plans didn't quite work out the way he'd envisioned. Instead, after being hit by a street car while walking downtown, he sued the city of Milwaukee and used the money to buy land in Fussville (now known as Menomonee Falls). There he established a farm where he grew vegetables and raised chickens, a few pigs, cows, and two beloved horses.

When their son Henry and his wife, Elinor, took over the farm, Elinor did most of the farming. Meanwhile, Henry, a talented salesman, handled produce sales. He wooed customers with catchphrases like "Step right up and get a bargain!" and his talents guided the farm through ten dark years during the Great Depression.

When third-generation Henry and his wife, Lynn, took over the farm in the 1970s, Henry took the role seriously. He pursued education in agriculture and streamlined farm operations. He also decided to focus the farm's production on greens, including collards, kale, and mustard greens. In addition to sales at local farmers markets, including the West Allis and Fondy Markets, he met with success selling to numerous local grocery stores, growing the farm's business in spades. But in the 1990s, things took a turn. Grocery store consolidation gave way to large chain stores and supercenters, and most grocers looked to national distribution for their produce. Consumer habits changed as well; everyone got busier, and fewer people took the time to cook. Local farms suffered.

It was a tough time, but things for the Centgraf family quickly got worse when their barn caught fire due to a faulty space heater. The losses were great and the farm never fully recovered. Meanwhile, the area around the farm erupted with suburban development, driving out all of the local farms. In the end, the Centgrafs didn't get much for their land, but it was enough to give them a fresh start in a new location.

In 2003, they purchased a forty-acre livestock farm in Mayville, Wisconsin, and started over. Henry planted a diverse range of vegetables using minimalist methods, including low-till planting, crop rotation, cover crops, mulching, trellising, hand weeding, and the use of only organic inputs. They raise bees for pollination and extend the growing season with frost blankets, low tunnels, and more recently a high tunnel. At first, Lynn took on a job in real estate to boost the income from the farm. By 2008, their daughter, Nicole, had graduated from college and was looking for a way to earn extra money. She connected with fruit farmers and started selling their fruits at the market. What began as a temporary job turned into a successful contribution to the family farm.

Around the same time, farmers markets had shifted gears, serving an increasing number of boutique shoppers who purchased less but were interested in a more varied selection of produce they couldn't find at the grocery store. So Centgraf began growing a variety of new crops, including heirloom tomatoes.

Restaurants were also solidly interested in purchasing vegetables, and they, too, wanted unique crops. Nicole had connections with a few restaurants in Milwaukee, including Wolf Peach and Hinterland (both of which

have since closed), that became the farm's first customers. The farm took cues based on chefs' needs and desires, growing crops like Badger Flame beets, scarlet frills mustard, rapini, heirloom squash varieties, and shelling beans. Word spread among chefs, and the farm acquired a new revenue stream.

Working with restaurants changed everything, not because restaurants were buying so much produce from the farm but because consumers were increasingly interested in new things, including heirloom vegetables. The crops the Centgrafs added to accommodate restaurants became a selling point for them at the farmers markets.

Centgraf Farms works with about twenty-five restaurants on a consistent basis, including the Bartolotta Restaurants, Third Coast Provisions, DanDan, and EsterEv, among others. Their success can be attributed to an emphasis on customer service and consistency, as well as the high quality of their varied produce.

During the pandemic, as income from restaurant sales waned, Centgraf launched a website to sell directly to consumers using a subscription-style service. It helped to grow their business during a time when staffing and costs for running the farm ran high.

Today the farm is run by third-generation owners Lynn and Henry Centgraf and their children Nicole, Henry, and Mat, each of whom plays an integral role in everyday operations. Together they take pride in watching their seeds grow, mature, and transform into delicious works of art, and they are encouraged by the support they receive from consumers and chefs who comment frequently on how delicious their vegetables are.

Steak Tartare with Shishito Peppers and Tomato

Chef Daniel Jacobs, EsterEv and DanDan with vegetables from Centgraf Farms

This party-worthy take on beef tartare is taken up a notch with the addition of umami-rich shishito pepper paste, farm-fresh tomatoes, and nutty pumpkin seeds. Chef Jacobs recommends serving the tartare with tortilla chips.

SERVES 4

For brine:

4 cups of water

2½ tablespoons kosher salt

For the beef:

6 ounces prime New York Strip

4 cups brine

For shishito paste:

½ pound shishito peppers

1 medium onion, cut into large chunks

8 garlic cloves

4 ounces shiro dashi or any other exceptional soy sauce

1 bunch cilantro leaves and stems

7 tablespoons toasted pumpkin seeds

3 tablespoons plus 2 teaspoons pumpkin seed oil

To prepare the brine:

A few hours before you want to make the tartare, make a 5 percent brine solution by heating 4 cups of water in a nonreactive pan. Add 2½ tablespoons of kosher salt and stir until dissolved. Cool the brine down thoroughly before using.

To prepare the beef:

Place the beef in the brine for 1 hour at room temperature. Pat dry and freeze for about 30 minutes or until it firms up. This makes the beef easier to cut into a small dice. Take your time and finely mince the steak. Set aside in your refrigerator until you are ready to assemble the dish.

To prepare the shishito paste:

On a grill (or over a gas flame), char the shishitos, onions, and garlic. You want a liberal amount of color on the outside of the vegetables; this develops flavor. After grilling, and while they are still hot, wrap the vegetables in plastic wrap to allow them to steam and finish cooking. Put vegetables, shiro dashi, cilantro stems and leaves, pumpkin seeds, and oil into the jar of a blender and blend well.

To prepare the tomatoes:

Prepare an ice bath. Bring a pot of salted water to a boil. Place tomatoes in the boiling water for 30 seconds, and then place immediately into the ice bath to stop the cooking. When cool, peel the tomatoes, cut them into quarters, and remove the seeds. Mince the tomato flesh and mix with rice wine vinegar, olive oil, and salt and pepper to taste.

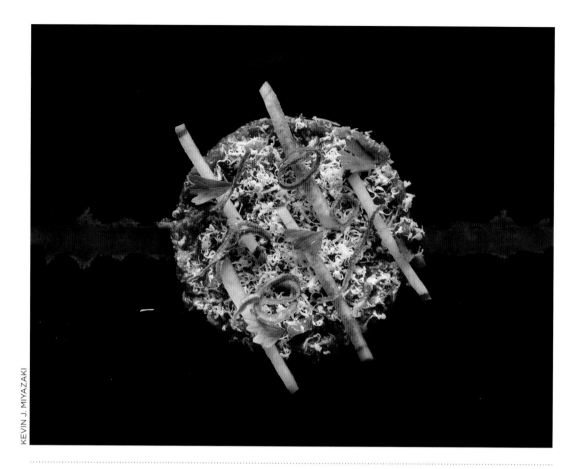

For tomatoes:

2 ripe tomatoes

1⅓ tablespoons rice wine vinegar

1⅓ tablespoons olive oil

kosher salt

pepper

For the garnish:

1 black or watermelon radish cut into matchsticks

a few cilantro leaves

fried tortillas, for serving

To assemble the tartare:

Mix minced beef with shishito pepper paste. Season with salt and pepper, to taste. You may want to add more pumpkin seed oil or dashi. Use your best judgment.

Split the meat between four plates using a 3-inch ring mold. Spoon tomatoes on top in an even layer and garnish with matchstick radishes and cilantro leaves.

Au Bon Canard

Caledonia, Minnesota
abcfoiegras.com

Tucked away among the rolling hills of southeastern Minnesota is Au Bon Canard, a sixty-acre duck farm where Christian Gasset and his wife, Liz Gibson-Gasset, raise between fifteen hundred and two thousand ducks per year, producing seasonal supply of their rich duck livers (foie gras), along with other cuts of duck for local consumption.

While most of the foie gras in the United States is produced by two duck farms in upstate New York (which produce as many as ten thousand ducks per week), the Gassets take a more hand-crafted approach, raising their pastured ducks in keeping with the French tradition without antibiotics, dietary supplements, appetite stimulants, or growth-promoting hormones.

A native of southwestern France, Christian was working as a logger in Africa when he met Liz. After he attended foie gras school in Perigord, France, the two decided to move to Minnesota and establish Au Bon Canard in 2001.

AU BON CANARD

AU BON CANARD

The ducks at Au Bon Canard spend most of their lives outside with plenty of sunshine and bugs to nibble. Moulard ducklings (a cross between Muscovy and Peking) are delivered to the farm when they are just a day old and nurtured in a heated, straw-lined room until their feathers have grown in and they can begin to spend time out of doors. From there, they move outside permanently, where they spend their days waddling around the farm, rotating through pastures amid horses and sheep to preserve the integrity of the land. As they grow, their feeding schedules are adjusted to prepare them for the gavage process, which begins when the ducks are about four months old. The process takes seconds, and Christian feeds the ducks one by one two times a day, increasing the amount of food daily for a duration of two weeks before they are prepared for slaughter and butchering.

Christian says three things are vital to Au Bon Canard's operation: respect for the birds, respect for the land, and respect for his customers. He believes in forming a connection to his ducks and maintaining a process that is as humane and as kind as possible. He also believes in maintaining transparency about his operation. Chefs and curious food lovers alike can make an appointment to tour the farm, walking through every step of a duck's life at Au Bon Canard.

Christian has a personal relationship with nearly all of his customers. Most are in Minnesota, but a few are restaurants that operate in Wisconsin and Illinois. Despite demand from chefs on the coasts, he wants to keep his business local and enjoys the opportunity to really get to know his customers. He has no desire to expand his business to meet demand; he prefers to maintain his current lifestyle, taking care of his ducks and caring for his land.

Foie Gras Mousse

Dan Bonanno,
A Pig in a Fur Coat
with foie gras from
Au Bon Canard

*Foie gras is an indulgence to be
savored on special occasions. Often
served in restaurants as a terrine or
torchon, this simple mousse from Chef
Dan Bonanno allows the luxurious
fattiness of farmer Christian Gasset's
duck liver to shine. Serve the mousse
with your choice of jam, fruit, or honey
and slices of toasted brioche. To take
things up another notch for your next
dinner party, tuck the mousse inside
mini choux pastry buns with a dab of
jam.*

SERVES 6

17½ ounces Grade A
  foie gras

½ cup Armagnac

2¼ teaspoons kosher
  salt

1¼ teaspoons sugar

½ cup heavy cream

Cut the raw foie gras into cubes and toss with Armagnac, salt, and sugar. Set aside and allow the liver to sit at room temperature for 10 minutes.

Place the foie gras in a food processor and blend, adding the heavy cream to create a smooth paste. Once blended, pass the mixture through a fine mesh sieve.

Transfer the mousse onto a large sheet of plastic wrap and roll it to form a 10–12-inch log. Roll the log as tightly as possible to eliminate any air bubbles. Rotate the log and place it onto another sheet of cling film. Roll it again, increasing the tightness of the roll. Secure each end of the roll with kitchen twine tied tightly into knots.

Place the log into the refrigerator overnight or until set.

Uplands Cheese

Dodgeville, Wisconsin
uplandscheese.com

Ask a cheesemaker how to create cheese with terroir and they will tell you: make cheese from the milk of one herd of cows, and make it only when they're consuming feed grown on that farm. Then age it with a natural rind that captures the flavors of that place.

It's a model that has worked well for Uplands Cheese, a farmstead creamery dedicated to the production of two raw milk cheeses: Pleasant Ridge Reserve, the most-awarded cheese in American history, and Rush Creek Reserve, an autumnal cheese available for just a few short months each year.

Owned and operated by Andy and Caitlin Hatch and Scott and Liana Mericka, Uplands Cheese is a family-run dairy farm and creamery sitting on three hundred acres in Dodgeville, Wisconsin. Its rolling hills are a natural habitat for grasslands, making it an ideal location

UPLANDS CHEESE

for an operation dedicated to responsible animal husbandry and land preservation.

Cows have been milked on the farm's rolling moors since the 1880s, but the farm's cheesemaking history began in the early 1990s when dairy farmers Dan Patenaude and Mike Gingrich purchased the farm and combined their respective herds. The two farmers were ahead of their time; they'd committed to rotational grazing in the 1980s because they saw the benefits, not only for their animals but also for the environment. Over time, they saw the fruits of their labor, and as they realized how flavorful their pasture-grazed milk was, they were inspired to use it for a higher purpose: making cheese.

Using that beautiful milk, Mike created the first wheels of Pleasant Ridge Reserve in 2000. Modeled after Alpine cheeses like Gruyere and Comte, which have been made with pasture-raised milk for hundreds of years, the washed-rind cheese is made during the summer months when the milk reflects the grassy flavors of the pastureland on the farm. It's a cheese that, aged for just four or five months, isn't very interesting, but when the fats and proteins are given time to break down, the flavor becomes more complex and reflects the quality of the milk itself.

In 2007, Andy Hatch joined Gingrich to assist in making Pleasant Ridge, a cheese that had already won accolades, including Best of Show

at the American Cheese Society's annual competition in 2001 and 2005 and honors as the winner of the U.S. Cheese Championships in 2003. Moving forward, the cheese would win Best of Show again in 2010, becoming the first cheese to win Best of Show three times and the only cheese to take home the prize in both major national cheese competitions.

A graduate of the dairy science program at the University of Wisconsin–Madison, Andy had also spent time working on local farms, as well as with cheesemakers in Europe, experiences that gave him valuable perspective on the relationships between the land, the animals, and the cheesemaking process.

In 2010, Scott moved across the country from California to assist with farming at Uplands. Despite his upbringing in a traditional farming family in North Carolina, he'd studied agronomy and grass-based dairy farming and quickly embraced the ideals inherent to the operations at Uplands.

In autumn of that same year, Andy—who had taken on more responsibility in Uplands cheesemaking—made the first batch of Rush Creek Reserve. Modeled after Vacherin Mont d'Or, a decadent seasonal cheese he'd had the honor of making while working in the Jura region of France, the cheese was a labor of love.

Rush Creek Reserve is made with the last milk of the season as the cows' diets transition from grass to hay. The milk is less flavorful and complex than its grassy summer counterpart. But what it lacks in flavor, it gains in weight and texture. Unlike Pleasant Ridge Reserve, which simply needs aging to bring out its flavor, Rush Creek Reserve benefits immensely from both ripening in spruce bark and the addition of yeasts and molds that create its flavor-giving rind. Although it varies from year to year, Rush Creek can always be counted on for its rich, creamy texture and a flavor that often carries hints of smoke, distinctive funk, and sometimes a whiff of rich, cured meats.

By 2014, as Dan and Mike welcomed the opportunity to step away from the farmstead, the Hatch and Mericka families purchased the farm, ensuring that it would continue for another generation.

KEVIN J. MIYAZAKI

Their combined efforts have ensured the continuity of two small-production (but highly decorated) cheeses, the reputations of which have created demand across the United States. Rush Creek Reserve, Pleasant Ridge Reserve, and Extra Aged Pleasant Ridge Reserve (aged at least fifteen months) are available on a limited basis for public consumption and purchase by restaurants through standard distribution channels.

While some restaurants prefer the efficiency of working with a distributor to source the cheeses, Uplands also deals directly with at least fifteen chefs who've cultivated personal relationships with the creamery. In some cases, those relationships play out in the form of midnight texts bearing special requests for wheels of cheese. In other cases, they provoke conversation about the characteristics of a particular batch of cheese and ways it can be worked into a menu. For those chefs who choose to make the extra effort, a trip to the creamery to taste through various batches of Pleasant Ridge Reserve could also result in the luck of sourcing a batch of cheese that's unique unto itself.

For some chefs, it's a point of pride that they can work directly with the creamery and its award-winning cheesemaker. But Andy says that sense of pride runs both ways: "It's an honor to work with so many talented local chefs."

Pleasant Ridge Reserve with Shallot Jam and Roasted Grapes

Chef Justin Aprahamian, Sanford Restaurant
with Pleasant Ridge Reserve from Uplands Cheese

This stunning appetizer showcases Uplands' Pleasant Ridge Reserve, the most awarded cheese in American history, pairing it with savory-sweet shallot jam and delectable roasted grapes. This appetizer takes time to make but is relatively easy to execute. If you're looking for a dish that's certain to impress, this one is a sure-fire win from one of Milwaukee's finest James Beard Award-winning chefs.

This dish may be accompanied by a small green salad.

SERVES 4

6 ounces Pleasant Ridge Reserve, divided into four pieces and brought to room temperature

For the shallot jam:

4 ounces shallots, thinly sliced

2 tablespoons olive oil

4 sprigs thyme

1 bay leaf

2½ tablespoons honey

2 tablespoons cider vinegar

½ teaspoon kosher salt

¼–½ teaspoon pepper

For the roasted grapes:

1 pound red seedless grapes

2 tablespoons extra virgin olive oil

salt and pepper, to taste

To prepare the shallot jam:

In a sauté pan, sweat the shallots and olive oil over medium heat until translucent (about 3–4 minutes). Add the thyme and bay leaf, and sauté 1 minute more. Add the honey and cider vinegar, and cook for 2 more minutes, being careful not to burn. Season with salt and pepper.

To prepare the grapes:

Preheat the oven to 375°F.

Wash the grapes and remove from stems, toss with the olive oil, and season to taste with salt and pepper. Toss the grapes into a hot, oven-proof pan and sauté for 1–2 minutes. Roast in the oven for 4–10 minutes, depending on size. Set aside half of the roasted grapes and liquid from the roasting pan for the grape reduction.

To prepare the grape reduction:

Place half of the roasted grapes in a strainer and push through to get juices. Combine with the reserved pan liquid. Dissolve the sugar and water in a saucepan and lightly caramelize. Carefully add the balsamic vinegar (it will boil violently). Reduce about halfway and add grape juice and reserved pan liquid. Bring to a boil and reduce to just under ½ cup. Season to taste with salt and pepper, and add a couple drops of lemon juice.

For the grape reduction:

half of the roasted grapes

reserved liquid from roasting
    pan

2 tablespoons sugar

2 tablespoons water

¼ cup balsamic vinegar

salt and pepper, to taste

few drops of lemon juice

To serve:

Divide the shallot jam among four plates. Top with the roasted grapes and cheese, and drizzle with grape reduction.

Daria Jean's Popovers with Pleasant Ridge Reserve Cheese

Chef Adam Siegel, Lupi & Iris
with Pleasant Ridge Reserve from Uplands Cheese

These flavorful popovers are a favorite in the Siegel household. They've become a signature item of Chef Adam Siegel's wife, Daria Jean, who will frequently surprise the family with warm fresh popovers to enjoy for breakfast.

Serve these beautifully airy popovers with flavored butter and wedges of Pleasant Ridge Reserve cheese or serve them alongside prime rib or other meaty entrees. In the autumn, when Rush Creek Reserve is available, take them to the next level by filling the airy centers with the indulgently gooey cheese for a truly memorable treat.

MAKES 6 LARGE OR
12 SMALL POPOVERS

- 1½ tablespoons unsalted butter, softened
- ½ ounce melted butter, unsalted
- 1½ cups all-purpose flour
- ¾ teaspoon kosher salt
- 3 extra large eggs
- 1½ cups whole milk
- 4 ounces Pleasant Ridge Reserve cheese

Preheat the oven to 425°F.

Butter the popover pans using the softened butter and heat them in the oven. Whisk together all the remaining ingredients, except for the cheese. The batter should be thin. Fill the popover pans less than half full. Divide the cheese among the tins and bake for approximately 30 minutes. Keep the oven door closed until the popovers are ready. Once they are baked, remove them from their tins and keep them warm by covering them with a kitchen towel.

LORI FREDRICH

Kaleidoscope Gardens

Milwaukee, Wisconsin
kaleidoscopegardens.com

It was 2014 when restaurant industry veteran Hannah Alabi transformed a vacant City of Milwaukee–owned lot into an intensively planted urban microfarm she named Kaleidoscope Gardens.

A lifelong gardener, Hannah earned a degree in environmental science, policy, and management from the University of Minnesota Twin Cities and pursued work as a naturalist for a few years. But it wasn't until her father passed away that she decided to pursue tangible work that combined her love for food, gardening, and environmental stewardship.

To prepare for what lay ahead, she worked as an intern with Loon Organics Farm in Minnesota, where she spent two seasons learning all she could about the science, business, and marketing involved in running a farm. Not only did she find farm work gratifying, but the physicality of the work also offered her a welcome distraction, during which she was able to focus on absorbing as much knowledge as possible from training

and volunteer opportunities that crossed her path.

In 2013, she made the move to Milwaukee, where she intentionally sought work at Braise, a restaurant she knew operated with a commitment to locally sourced food. While there, she established Kaleidoscope Garden, selling on a small scale to Braise and building connections with additional restaurants in the area. Soon she began dipping her toe into consumer sales, and by 2016 she was selling weekly at farmers markets as well as local restaurants.

Today, Kaleidoscope Gardens comprises approximately one and a half acres of intensely planted organic gardens, including land in Oak Creek and Downtown Milwaukee and a hoop house in South Milwaukee, which has been retrofitted to function as a greenhouse for growing starter plants and extending the growing season for select plants.

Crops include a diverse collection of culinary herbs and vegetables, including peppers, zucchini, and both summer and winter squash, which she supplements with specialty crops often grown at the request of restaurant chefs. In addition to growing with care for the soil, Hannah says she has developed systems for postharvest handling, which ensure that the produce lasts for an extended period of time.

Six years after launching her business, Hannah still finds the work extraordinarily gratifying. Not only is it variable and flexible, but it has also allowed her to exercise creativity and engage in collaboration with a community of urban growers and the chefs and workers in Milwaukee's restaurant community. It's work she sees as both a science and an art form, a never-ending journey of learning, growing, and sharing.

Chive Blossom Biscuits

Chef Nathan Heck and Laura Maigatter, Hot Dish Pantry with herbs from Kaleidoscope Gardens

This biscuit recipe is both versatile and simple. There's no butter pinching, and you can modify it with different herbs to suit your taste. You can also freeze the dough and bake it later to preserve the flavor of spring.

One key to this recipe is keeping the butter as cold as possible for as long as possible. The other key is moving as quickly as possible, which ensures that you're keeping the butter cold. Be sure to read through the entire recipe and then read through it again before removing the grated butter from the freezer. It's also easiest if you draw up the cutting guide before you make the dough.

MAKES 8 BISCUITS

For the butter:

1½ sticks butter (chilled)

2¼ cups all-purpose flour, plus more for dusting

3 tablespoons melted butter for brushing

For the biscuits:

½ teaspoons baking soda

1¾ teaspoons baking powder

1¾ teaspoons sugar

2¼ teaspoons kosher salt

½ teaspoons black pepper

½ teaspoons mustard powder

½ teaspoons garlic powder

8 chive blossom tops (remove purple blossoms from the stem and flower base)

1¼ cups sour cream

To prepare the butter and the pan:

Chill the butter in the freezer for at least 1 hour. Make a cutting guide by taking a piece of parchment and drawing a roughly 4 × 8 inch rectangle on one side. Make lines down the center in both directions, extending the lines past the edge of the rectangle by about an inch. Flip that over and place the parchment paper in the bottom of a sheet pan. This will be your guide when you begin cutting.

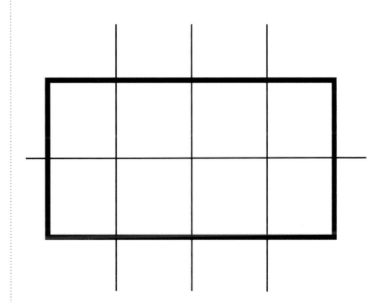

Generously sprinkle the parchment-lined sheet tray with flour. Using a cheese grater, grate the chilled butter over the tray, pausing regularly to toss the newly grated butter with flour to coat.

Place the flour-coated grated butter back into the freezer while preparing dry ingredients.

Melt 3 tablespoons butter on stovetop and keep handy.

To prepare the biscuits:

Preheat the oven to 425°F.

Combine flour, baking soda and powder, sugar, salt, pepper, mustard powder, garlic, and chive blossoms in a large bowl and whisk evenly to incorporate. Remove grated butter from the freezer and toss it in the bowl with the dry ingredients. Keep the parchment-lined tray handy.

Add the sour cream and begin incorporating it into the flour. Continue until the dough begins to come together but is still very shaggy. You do not want the dough to become soggy. If you can take a clump of dough in your fist and it sticks together, you are good to go.

To layer the biscuits:

When the dough is still very shaggy, turn it out onto the parchment-lined tray and begin to shape into a rectangle. Use the edges of the parchment to aid in shaping the sides of the dough into a rough rectangle about 4 × 8 inches. Do not worry if you have a bunch of dry schnibbles (or small scraps) scattered around. They will be incorporated in the layering process.

Cut the rectangle in half, scoop up the dry pieces and place them on top of one side, and then layer the other side over the one with the schnibbles, sandwiching the schnibbles in between. A bench scraper makes this process much easier. Then smash the two sides to flatten into another roughly 4 × 8 inch rectangle. Feel free to use a rolling pin for this part. Don't worry if you have pieces falling around—you will neaten the block after the layering is over.

Repeat the layering process one more time and then clean up the edges and make sure your final shape is roughly 4 × 8 inches and is level on top. Place your hand under the parchment and press into the sides of the rectangle to sharpen the edges. Try to center your rectangle over the guide you created at the beginning.

Cut the dough into eight biscuits. First cut it in half lengthwise, and then cut the new thin rectangles in half. Cut these in half again, making eight roughly 2 × 2 inch biscuits. This is much easier using the guidelines you created earlier. Once they are cut, place them 2 inches apart on the parchment and put the sheet pan into the freezer to set the butter.

Once they have chilled for at least 10 minutes, they can go straight into the oven or be packaged to cook from frozen later. Brush the biscuits with melted butter before placing them in the oven. Bake for 18–22 minutes or until dark golden brown. Brush again with melted butter right after they are out of the oven. Sprinkle lightly with sea salt.

To bake biscuits from frozen:

Follow the cooking instructions above, but bake for 21–25 minutes or until dark golden brown.

PepperRich Farm

Milwaukee, Wisconsin
pepperrichfarm.com

In 2019, James Michael Arms decided to make a leap into the agricultural arena, establishing an urban farm that specializes in rare varieties of peppers and other esoteric plants.

Michael, who grew up in Knoxville, Tennessee, says he was always prone to collecting. Throughout his childhood, he accumulated comic books, rocks, shells, and even ceramic dogs and cats. It's a tendency that he links to his current obsession with cultivating myriad unusual peppers.

An artist by trade, Michael studied at the Atlanta College of Art before moving to Los Angeles to work in film. In California, he took up organic gardening. When a work assignment took him to Brazil, he remained there for over a decade before moving to Milwaukee, Wisconsin, at the behest of a friend.

After arriving in The Cream City in 2016, he took a job at C-Viche, a restaurant specializing in Ibero-American fare from climes including Mexico, Peru, and South America. It was there that he began to take note of the relative rarity of peppers he'd encountered while living in Brazil. Varieties like the aji charapita, a tiny Peruvian pepper with a fruity, floral flavor and a moderate bite, were difficult to source in the United States and were, as a result, relatively unknown by those without a connection to South America. Intrigued, he began growing rare varieties of peppers on the patio at the restaurant.

The more peppers he grew, the more intrigued he became. Eventually, his collector mentality kicked in, and he expanded to a community garden plot, where he experimented with as many as forty-five to fifty different peppers to see what would flourish. A basic knowledge of gardening paired with natural curiosity led him to YouTube videos and gardening groups, from which he gleaned information that informed his new hobby.

Along the way, he discovered what he liked and what he didn't, settling on peppers that delivered on big flavor profiles and not just heat.

After growing at the community garden for three years, it became evident that a greenhouse would be necessary. Fortunately, Michael had connected with Erin Dentice, creator of the agriculture program at Parkside School for the Arts, who hooked him up with a 20 × 70 foot hoop house on city-owned land where Parkside maintains a few of its gardens, along with farms like Kaleidoscope Gardens and A&M Organics.

Today, Michael farms part-time, growing upward of 350 plants, including twenty-five to thirty different peppers and other unusual plants, including herbs like huacatay (black mint), a giant variety of marigold that's native to the Andes in South America. His urban farm employs organic practices, utilizing local sources for compost and water from a nearby cistern.

He's also adapted the hoop house to include a smaller tent-like structure, electric heaters, and a heated water system that helps to maintain a higher soil temperature around his plants. The systems allow him to keep the plants alive year-round, taking advantage of the perennial nature of the peppers to produce larger harvests.

It's not surprising that chefs were among the first to take interest in PepperRich Farm's peppers. Creative chefs including Ross Bachhuber from Odd Duck, Paul Zerkel at Goodkind, and Nathan Heck of Hot Dish Pantry have all purchased seasonal fruits to experiment with at their restaurants.

But in an effort to find better ways to use and preserve a larger number of peppers, Michael began making single-variety hot sauces, which showcase the individual flavor profiles of each pepper. Currently, he makes more than a dozen types of hot sauces, including a sriracha-style sauce using aji angelo, a pepper with medium heat levels but a sweet, fruity flavor and excellent aromatics. The sauces are sold limitedly to restaurants but are also available to the public via retail establishments like Lion's Tooth bookstore.

Currently, Michael says he's honing in on which peppers produce the best, and which varieties lend themselves best to particular uses. He's also focused on improving the irrigation methods used at the farm. On the business side, he's finding better ways to market his peppers—and share his pepper-filled passion—in a more impactful way.

Tomato Huacatay Jam

Chef Nathan Heck and Laura Maigatter, Hot Dish Pantry
with huacatay from PepperRich Farm

Huacatay (wah-ka-tay) is a beautifully aromatic plant that's native to the Andes in South America. It is also known as Peruvian black mint, mint marigold, wild marigold, or Mexican marigold. It's a relatively rare find, but Michael Arms of PepperRich Farm cultivates this herb on his small urban farm in Milwaukee, Wisconsin. Its flavor is reminiscent of a mix of tarragon, sweet basil, and mint.

Huacatay is also available in dried form or as a paste; either form will work well in this recipe. However, if you'd like, you can replace the huacatay with another fresh herb.

This tomato jam is a lovely addition to the Chive Blossom Biscuits in this book (page 27). But you can also enjoy it with a fried egg on toast, add it to your next cheese board, or use it to add a bit of sweet herbal flavor to a burger. Feel free to let your imagination run wild. There are no rules.

SAMANTHA SANDRIN

MAKES 1 PINT

- 1 cup granulated sugar
- 1 tablespoon huacatay (or tarragon and/or mint, basil, or other herbs)
- ½ teaspoon kosher salt
- ½ teaspoon black pepper
- ½ teaspoon chili flakes
- ¼ teaspoon dried ginger powder
- ⅛ teaspoon nutmeg
- 1½ pounds of fresh tomatoes, cored, small to medium diced
- 1 lemon, juiced (small to medium)

Combine the sugar with the herbs and spices.

In a nonstick pot, combine the dry ingredients with the tomatoes and lemon juice and bring to a boil over medium-high heat, stirring often. Reduce heat and simmer until mixture reaches a thick, jam-like consistency, making sure to stir often. This process usually takes about 1½–2 hours.

Use the spoon test to gauge when your jam is done. Just dip a chilled spoon into the mix and tilt the spoon over the pot. If the jam comes off in drips, it is not done. When it comes off in a sheet, the jam is finished. If you are unsure, let it go a little longer, especially if you prefer a slightly thicker jam over a thin, runny one.

Charapita Hot Honey

Chef Nathan Heck and Laura Maigatter, Hot Dish Pantry with peppers from PepperRich Farm

Hot honey is among Chef Nathan Heck and Laura Maigatter's favorite toppings for eggs, pizza, and biscuits. It also happens to be a condiment that's easy to make and modify according to taste. Prefer it a bit on the hotter side? Add more hot sauce. No citrus in the house? Use apple cider vinegar. Easy.

This signature hot honey is made using a single varietal PepperRich Farm hot sauce made with aji charapita peppers. The South American peppers are tiny in size, but they deliver a big punch. Incorporating them into honey allows their subtle fruity flavors to bloom and rounds out the heat. If you can't find aji charapita peppers or hot sauce, home or farm-grown habaneros make a fine substitute.

YIELDS 1 CUP

1 cup local wildflower honey

2 teaspoons charapita hot sauce

¼ teaspoon lemon zest

¼ teaspoon orange zest

2 star anise pods

½ teaspoon chili flakes

¼ teaspoon whole fennel seeds

⅛ teaspoon salt

⅛ teaspoon black pepper

Add all ingredients to a pot and bring to a simmer over medium heat. Simmer for about 5 minutes, as this process allows the dried herbs and spices to bloom. Remove from the heat and allow the honey to cool to room temperature. Once the honey has cooled, stir a few times to make sure the flavors are incorporated.

Store in a clean glass jar, straining out the spices and zest if desired.

Wickman House Garden

Ellison Bay, Wisconsin
wickmanhouse.com

The Door County Peninsula, often called the "Cape Cod of the Midwest," is known for its picturesque coastal towns, fish boils, and bountiful cherry and apple orchards. But despite its agricultural underpinnings, its short growing season and rocky, sandy soil make it a challenging place to grow food. And yet, when Mike Holmes opened Wickman House in 2012, his goal was to create a restaurant where at least 50 percent of every plate contained produce that was grown right on the peninsula. The best way to ensure that, of course, was to establish a large-scale garden from which they could harvest fresh produce during the growing season.

The original Wickman crew cleared the land for its first garden plot, transforming a field of depleted soil into a more fertile landscape where they grew crops like peppers, tomatoes, kale, and collard greens. In time, lead gardeners Adam Prugh and Mattea Fischer set up systems for

watering, built a greenhouse for starting plants, and expanded the garden to include flowers and raised beds.

Today the garden is operated in part by Kaitlyn Newberry, an artist whose interest in creating with natural materials offered her a creative entry into agriculture. She took over operations at the Wickman Garden in 2019 when her husband, Cooper, took on a role as line chef at Wickman House, eventually working his way up to co-head chef at their sister restaurant, Trixie's, in 2022.

Beginning with the 2022 season, Wickman House also brought on Tom Horsley, a landscaper turned farmer who serves as both mentor and co-leader with the goal of expanding the produce grown for the restaurant.

Currently, Kaitlyn and Tom are working hard to promote soil health in the garden. To do so, they use a no-till system that uses organic methods, including composting and crop rotation, to increase production in the relatively small garden. They also implement permaculture, interspersing herbs and flowers between the vegetable crops to promote the health of the plants and reduce pests.

XOME STUDIO

They work closely with the chefs to ensure that there's synergy between what's grown in the garden and the dishes on the menu. Each spring, the garden team meets with the chefs to plan the plantings for the season, focusing on unique produce varieties, as well as crops that grow particularly well, like broccolini, radishes, beets, and carrots.

During the growing season, the restaurants' ever-changing menus are created based on what's coming out of the garden, as well as what's available from other local farms. The focus each year is on increasing the quality of the produce that's harvested. The ultimate goal is to create more of a chef's garden that can grow specific varieties of vegetables that not only meet the needs for the kitchens at both Wickman House and Trixie's but also allow the chefs to push the boundaries of their creativity to deliver unique, hyperlocal cuisine.

Gluten-Free Tempura Spring Onions

The chef team at Trixie's
with fresh vegetables from the Wickman House Garden

Boring onion rings, be gone. These sexy, ultra-crisp spring onions make a fantastic bar snack or vegan starter, especially paired with zippy horseradish aioli. Enjoy them with a craft brew or cocktail in hand.

SERVES 4-6

For the horseradish aioli:

½ cup aioli (see recipe on page 40)

1 tablespoon ketchup

2 tablespoons horseradish

¼ teaspoon paprika

¼ teaspoon kosher salt

¼ teaspoon garlic powder

⅛ teaspoon oregano

For the tempura batter and onions:

grapeseed or another neutral oil, for frying

½ cup rice flour

⅓ cup potato starch

¼ cup tapioca flour

½ teaspoon baking powder

¾ cup ice water

1 bunch green onions, cleaned and stems trimmed down (onions should have small to medium bulbs, ensuring that they cook through)

To prepare the horseradish aioli:

Mix together ½ cup of homemade aioli with remaining ingredients. Whisk until smooth. Set aside.

To prepare the tempura spring onions:

Fill a deep fryer with oil and preheat to 350°F. Alternatively, pour enough oil into a 6-quart Dutch oven (or large, deep pot) to reach a depth of 2 inches. Heat the oil until a deep-fry thermometer reads 350°F.

Make the tempura batter by mixing the rice flour, potato starch, tapioca flour, baking powder, and ice water until it's smooth.

Working in batches (if needed), dip the green onions into the batter and carefully place into the frying oil. Fry for 1-2 minutes, and then flip and fry for an additional 1-2 minutes or until crispy and golden brown. Salt once the onions come out of fryer oil and serve with the horseradish aioli.

Easy Aioli

These days the word *aioli* is often used interchangeably with garlicky mayonnaise, although the condiments are quite distinctive. Traditional Mediterranean aioli is made with three simple ingredients: olive oil, garlic, and salt, which have been laboriously emulsified with a mortar and pestle. Due to the labor required and the fact that the emulsion breaks easily, updated versions often use egg yolks to stabilize the emulsion. This easy version can be made in 5 minutes or less.

MAKES 1 CUP

1 whole egg
4 cloves garlic, minced
2 teaspoons freshly squeezed lemon juice
½ cup neutral oil like grapeseed
½ cup high-quality extra virgin olive oil
kosher salt

Combine the egg, garlic, and lemon juice in a food processor. With the machine running, slowly drizzle in the grapeseed oil, scraping down the sides as needed. Transfer the mixture to a medium bowl. Whisking constantly, slowly drizzle the extra virgin olive oil into the egg mixture until well combined. Season to taste with salt. The aioli will keep for up to two weeks stored in the refrigerator in an airtight container.

Yuppie Hill Poultry

Burlington, Wisconsin
yuppiehillpoultry.com

Due to processing time, eggs can be two to three weeks old by the time they reach the shelves in the grocery store. That's not the case with eggs from Yuppie Hill Poultry, a small local farm in Walworth County, Wisconsin, that raises cage-free, vegetarian-fed eggs delivered to local grocers and restaurants less than twenty-four hours after harvest. It's a pride point for Lynn Lein, who founded Yuppie Hill in 2001 with a flock of just twelve laying hens.

Lynn had always wanted to farm. Having spent summers growing up working on a friend's dairy farm, she thought her passion might land her in the dairy industry. But the realization that she needed a farm that she could run on her own made her shift gears. So she left the city and moved her family to a home in Burlington, Wisconsin.

For years, Lynn talked about wanting a few backyard chickens. One day, when her son Jay was a senior in high school, he surprised her by bringing home twelve hens. Initially, they kept the flock in their horse barn. But when they built them a formal chicken coop, Lynn fancied up the space with wallpaper, curtains, and flower boxes on the windows. No one in their rural area had a chicken coop quite like it. When neighbors would visit, they'd often comment on the chickens' clean, "upscale" quarters, referring to Lynn and her sons as the "yuppies on the hill."

The name stuck. When the farm reached a capacity that allowed it, they began selling their fresh eggs at the local farmers market under the name Yuppie Hill Poultry.

When Lynn first started farming, there weren't many cage-free systems available, so Yuppie Hill was among the first mid-size farms to use aviary systems. And despite growth, they've remained true to their standards, investing in high-quality feed supplemented with omega-3 fatty acids and providing a habitat for their hens that offers them space to move, peck, and do all the things chickens naturally do.

The rich flavor of the well-formed, rich yolks brought customers back, and word of mouth was the only form of advertising needed to bring new business to the swiftly growing farm. Yuppie Hill's inaugural dozen chickens soon grew to a flock of three hundred, and they acquired more land at a farm just five miles from their homestead. As they expanded, demand grew to include local restaurants and small grocers, including their very first customer, Beans & Barley, a specialty grocer and restaurant on Milwaukee's East Side that remains among their most loyal buyers.

Today, despite the rising costs and staff shortages that have challenged farms across the nation, Yuppie Hill has persisted. They currently deliver their eggs to over thirty restaurants and grocers, while maintaining a growing waiting list of eager customers.

Lynn admits that farming has become a more stressful proposition in recent years, but she says she loves the independence that farming affords, as well as the satisfaction that comes with knowing that customers continue to value their high-quality eggs.

Her love of caring for animals drives her forward. Bringing in a new flock of "girls" is among her favorite chores. She loves overseeing the hard work of preparing the barn, cleaning and power-washing the girls' new home; she welcomes the exciting new challenges that come with getting to know a new flock of birds, all of which exhibit their own distinctive personalities.

But her greatest satisfaction comes in the form of being able to work side-by-side with her children, along with the pride of knowing that her popular egg business is successful enough to support six families.

Spanish Tortilla

Chef Dave Swanson, Braise Restaurant
with eggs from Yuppie Hill Poultry

For Chef Dave Swanson, the Spanish tortilla, a classic tapas dish, is often the inaugural dish that kicks off the depravity of countless food-filled nights during his travels in Spain. When he put the dish on the menu at Braise, his goal was to highlight locally raised eggs as a starring protein in a dish that wasn't relegated to brunch.

Serve this dish as a main course with a beautiful green salad or enjoy—as they would in Spain—alongside an afternoon gin and tonic on the patio.

SERVES 3 AS A MAIN COURSE;
SERVES 6 AS AN APPETIZER

3 Yukon Gold potatoes, peeled and sliced

2 tablespoons extra virgin olive oil

kosher salt and pepper, to taste

12 Yuppie Hill Poultry eggs

½ cup half and half cream

3 garlic cloves, minced

1 cup fresh goat cheese

Preheat the oven to 350°F.

In a cast-iron pan, sauté potatoes in olive oil over medium heat until tender and golden brown. Season with salt and pepper and set aside. In a medium bowl, mix eggs, cream, and garlic until combined. Season with salt and pepper. In the same cast-iron pan, create alternating layers of potato and cheese. Top with egg mixture after each layer. Repeat until all ingredients are used. Bake in the oven for 30 minutes, until the tortilla is set and golden brown on top. Remove from heat and let cool; serve at room temperature.

Alsum Sweet Corn

Randolf, Wisconsin
alsumsweetcorn.com

The Alsum Sweet Corn story begins—surprisingly—on a dairy farm. New-lyweds Harvey and Elizabeth Alsum had purchased the farm in 1912 and milked cows there for over fifty years. When they sold the farm to their son Ken and his wife, Myrna, the tradition continued.

But it was a fateful day in the spring of 1976 when Ken planted his first field of sweet corn. His hope was to establish a new crop that he could sell to consumers at the newly minted Dane County Farmers Market. He had no idea at the time whether he'd meet with success, but the notion of connecting with market customers and delivering fresh local produce to them was an exciting prospect.

The first year's crop was sold roadside by his oldest son, Scott, who took on the role of delivering corn to area grocers and farm stands, eventually landing a vendor stall at the Dane County Market in 1981. By the mid-1990s, the corn business had taken off and Ken decided to give up dairy farming altogether. Alsum Sweet Corn was here to stay.

In 2009, Scott and his wife, Lona, purchased the family farm, where they now live with their five children: Ben, Brittany, Luke, Levi, and Lily.

Ben and Levi both work full-time on the farm, which grows a hundred acres of non-GMO sweet corn, a hundred acres of pumpkins, twenty acres of squash, and additional acreage for edible crops including green beans, yellow beans, sugar snap peas, cucumbers, pickles, zucchini, and kohlrabi. Ben, the entrepreneur of the family, had also pushed for including straw-berries and cabbage, which were both added in the past two years.

Lona, who manages the books for the farm, also oversees Alsum's on-site commercial kitchen, where sweet corn is processed, packaged, and frozen for sale during the off-season. Packaged corn products include bi-color, yellow, white, bi-color with sweet pepper medley, bi-color with jalapeños, and bi-color with cherry bomb peppers.

Their corn and vegetables can be found on the shelves of local grocers, including Piggly Wiggly, Metcalfe's Market, and Outpost Natural Foods, as well as at five seasonal roadside stands and various summer and winter farmers markets, including the Dane County Farmers Market where they started over forty years ago.

Alsum sweet corn is also a popular product among chefs in the Madison and Milwaukee markets, appearing on menus at multiunit restaurants like Forage Kitchen and Ian's Pizza along with eateries like Morris Ramen in Madison, Braise in Milwaukee, I.d. in Delafield, and Tumbled Rock Brewery & Kitchen in Baraboo.

Scott says they've connected with most restaurants through the farmers markets, so personal relationships with chefs are common. He takes care to keep in touch through weekly texts, letting them know what's available for sale and delivering it later in the week. He considers his work with restaurants some of the most gratifying, since he can get feedback about their produce firsthand as well as witness the creative ways that chefs make use of their products.

Farming is definitely challenging, but Scott likes the freedom to work outdoors, spend quality time with family, and meet people who genuinely appreciate what they grow. These rewards make getting up every morning and going to work worth it.

Elote Flatbread

Chef Joe Heppe, l.d. at the Delafield Hotel
with corn from Alsum Sweet Corn

This dish started as a way to showcase corn in a creative way. But the recipe evolved, and the chef team began adding huitlacoche puree, using locally grown "corn smut" from local forager Mushroom Mike, taking the flatbread to the next level.

If you can't find huitlacoche (a flavorful mushroom-like fungus that grows on corn), feel free to make the recipe without the huitlacoche puree. It will still be delicious.

Note: The flatbread recipe that follows makes enough for a crowd. Wrap the par-cooked flatbreads well, and they can be stored in the freezer for up to three months. Thaw them before baking for a convenient appetizer or personal pizza.

SERVES 4 AS AN APPETIZER

For the corn sauce:

½ cup olive oil

1 medium Vidalia onion, diced

3 garlic cloves, smashed

1 teaspoon smoked paprika

¼ teaspoon turmeric

pinch of crushed red pepper flakes

2 cups shucked corn kernels

2 cups vegetable stock

kosher salt, to taste

For the huitlacoche puree:

½ cup olive oil

1 medium Vidalia onion, diced

½ cup shiitake mushroom, thinly sliced

8 cloves black garlic

1 cup huitlacoche, frozen

½ teaspoon dried epazote

1 tablespoon sherry vinegar

1 quart vegetable or mushroom stock

kosher salt, to taste

To prepare the corn sauce:

Sweat the onions and garlic in olive oil on medium heat until soft and tender, lightly caramelized. Add the smoked paprika, turmeric, and red pepper flakes. Cook for 2 minutes, stirring regularly. Add the corn and season with salt; cook on medium for 10 minutes, stirring regularly. Add the vegetable stock and simmer for 10 minutes. Blend using a blender or hand blender; puree the corn with as little cooking liquid as needed until you achieve a smooth consistency. Adjust seasoning with salt. Set aside. You will likely have enough sauce to make multiple flatbreads.

To prepare the huitlacoche puree:

Sweat the onions in olive oil on medium heat until soft and tender, and lightly caramelized. Add the shiitake mushrooms and cook on medium heat until soft. Add the black garlic, huitlacoche, epazote, sherry vinegar, and just enough mushroom or vegetable stock to cover the vegetables. Simmer for 10 minutes. Blend using a blender or hand blender until you have a thick puree with a smooth consistency. Adjust seasoning with salt. Place in a squeeze bottle and reserve in a warm space until flatbreads are ready for finishing.

For the chipotle aioli:

1 cup aioli or mayo

1½ tablespoon chipotle in adobo sauce puree

1 tablespoon lime juice

Cheeses:

1 cup Carr Valley Mellage cheese, coarsely grated

1 cup cotija cheese, finely grated

Finishing ingredients:

¼ cup pickled corn (use your favorite recipe)

¼ cup pickled red onion

reserved cotija cheese

1 caramelized lime (see recipe for preparation)

micro cilantro or freshly chopped cilantro leaves

Note: Leftover puree will keep in the refrigerator for four to five days; use as a flavor booster for corn on the cob, nachos, quesadillas, or tacos—or even as a sauce for steak.

To prepare the chipotle aioli:

Mix all ingredients together. Place in a squeeze bottle and keep in the refrigerator until the flatbread comes out of the oven.

To caramelize your limes:

Slice the limes in half and dip the cut side in sugar. Using a crème brûlée torch, caramelize the sugar on the cut side of the lime. Set aside for plating.

To prepare previously baked flatbreads:

Preheat the oven to 450°F.

Brush flatbread with olive oil, spoon on a generous portion of the corn sauce, using the back of the spoon to evenly spread. Sprinkle the Mellage cheese and half of the cotija evenly on the flatbread, making sure to get some cheese on the crust. Bake until the cheese is golden brown (5–8 minutes).

Once flatbread comes out of the oven, garnish with pickled corn and onions, reserved cotija cheese, a swirl of chipotle aioli and huitlacoche puree, a squeeze of caramelized lime, and cilantro.

Flatbread Dough

3 cups finely ground whole-wheat flour (preferably Indian atta or King Arthur whole-wheat)

1 teaspoon kosher salt

½ cup olive oil, divided

1½ cups water

Preheat the oven to 425°F.

Stir together flour, salt, and 2 tablespoons of oil in a large bowl. Slowly stir in water until a soft dough forms. If necessary, add more water, 1 tablespoon at a time. Turn out dough onto a lightly floured surface and knead, dusting with just enough flour to keep dough from sticking, until smooth and elastic (about 15 minutes).

Form dough into a ball and coat with 2 tablespoons of oil in a bowl. Cover bowl with plastic wrap and let dough stand at warm room temperature 1 hour.

Divide the dough into twelve equal pieces; keeping remaining pieces covered with plastic wrap, flatten one piece of dough into a disk. Roll out the disk as thinly as possible into a 9-inch round on a lightly floured surface with a 6-inch wooden dowel or a rolling pin. Transfer to a large sheet of parchment paper, and then loosely cover with plastic wrap until you are ready to bake.

Make remaining flatbreads in the same manner.

Brush flatbreads with olive oil. Bake until the dough just starts to turn gold. Remove and let chill to room temp, apply toppings of choice, and then return to the oven until the crust turns golden brown and the cheese (if used) is melted.

Soups, Salads, and Sides

Recipes

JERRY'S PRODUCE

Featured Farms

Jerry's Produce

New Berlin, Wisconsin
facebook.com/JerrysProduceWI

Growing things came naturally for Jerry Wagner. He grew up dabbling with plants, helping out on a friend's family orchard, and taking on various gardening projects of his own. It was his appreciation for the growing cycle that transforms a seed into a fruit-bearing plant that hooked him for life.

For many years, he farmed on a part-time basis, growing squash, peppers, and tomatoes and selling the produce at the West Allis Farmers Market. He started with a small plot of family land, but eventually he began renting land from others. In 2012, he and his wife, Paula, decided to take on farming as a full-time profession.

Today, Jerry's Produce farms between twelve and fifteen acres each season, growing more than a hundred kinds of produce and selling directly to consumers and restaurants through both the New Berlin and the West

JERRY'S PRODUCE

HOOT BLOSSOM FARM

Allis farmers markets. Over the years, they've become well known for crops such as garlic (of which they grow up to eight varieties), along with various peppers and tomatoes.

Among the pleasures of Jerry and Paula's weekly trips to the market is engaging customers in conversation about the food they grow and introducing them to vegetables that they've never tried before. Years of one-on-one conversations have earned them a loyal market following of regular customers and, ultimately, friends.

JERRY'S PRODUCE

But their work with local restaurants has also become a gratifying part of their farming experience, exposing them to a larger audience of eaters and offering them the opportunity to see the food they've grown transformed into a literal picture on a plate.

For years, they've worked with a slate of local chefs—including Jonathan Manyo at Morel, Thi Cao of Wild Roots, and Kyle Knall of Birch—occasionally growing custom items for restaurants when the demand is high enough. The farm also started a winter storage program explicitly for restaurants and has extended the season for some crops to ensure that they can source fresh produce longer. Farm deliveries take place primarily during the winter months, but most chefs pick up their produce directly from the market during the summer months when new crops are coming in on a weekly basis.

For Jerry, it's about maintaining relationships with the chefs, understanding their needs, and getting to know them. In most cases, relationships extend well beyond simple business transactions, evolving into long-term friendships built on good communication and a love for fresh, local food.

Chilled Buttermilk Cucumber Soup

Chef Thi Cao, Wild Roots
with cucumbers from Jerry's Produce

Farm-fresh cucumbers are the base for this refreshing summer soup that gleans depth from tangy buttermilk and bright vegetal notes from the addition of fresh herbs. Serve as a summer starter or a light lunch.

SERVES 4-6

For the soup:

3 cucumbers, peeled and diced

¼ medium yellow onion, diced

2 cups buttermilk

2 tablespoons chopped fresh mint

2 tablespoons chopped fresh dill

2 garlic cloves, minced

½ of one jalapeño pepper, seeded and ribbed

2 tablespoons lemon juice

1 tablespoon rice wine vinegar or champagne vinegar

freshly ground black pepper

kosher salt

1–3 tablespoons of sorghum syrup or honey, to taste

1 tablespoon extra virgin olive oil

For the garnish:

3 hard-boiled eggs, whites separated from the yolks and chopped

¼ cup croutons

fresh mint, chopped

fresh dill, chopped

extra virgin olive oil

To prepare the soup:

Combine cucumbers, onion, buttermilk, mint, dill, garlic, jalapeño, lemon juice, and vinegar in the jar of a blender and blend until smooth. Season with salt and pepper to taste, and add the sorghum syrup or honey if the soup could use a bit of sweetness. Then add the olive oil and blend on high to emulsify.

Chill immediately. For best flavor, allow the soup to sit in the refrigerator overnight or up to 48 hours. The soup will keep for up to a week in the refrigerator.

To serve:

Pour the soup into a chilled bowl and garnish with boiled chopped eggs, croutons, herbs, and a drizzle of extra virgin olive oil.

Roasted Pumpkin Soup with Toasted Pumpkin Seeds and Caramelized Pumpkin

Chef Justin Aprahamian, Sanford
with pumpkin from Jerry's Produce

Warm soup is a treat as the weather grows cooler, and this pumpkin soup from Chef Justin Aprahamian checks all the boxes, incorporating warming spices and roasted pumpkin. Nutty toasted pumpkin seeds and deliciously caramelized pumpkin add depth and interest to the pureed soup.

SERVES 6-8

For the roasted pumpkin:

1 pumpkin (~4 pounds)

3 generous tablespoons butter

For the caramelized pumpkin:

2 tablespoons butter

2 teaspoons olive oil

¼ of the pumpkin, peeled, medium dice

kosher salt and pepper, to taste

2-3 tablespoons honey

4 teaspoons vinegar (more to taste)

For the pumpkin seeds:

¼ cup pumpkin seeds

olive oil, to lightly coat

kosher salt and pepper, to taste

To prepare the pumpkin:

Preheat the oven to 375°F.

Wash and cut the pumpkin in quarters. Scrape seeds out with a large spoon. Put a tablespoon of butter on three of the quarters, reserving one quarter for caramelized pumpkin garnish.

Place on cookie sheet and roast in oven for 30–40 minutes or until golden brown and tender. When cool enough to handle, remove skin and discard. Reserve roasted pumpkin meat.

To prepare the caramelized pumpkin:

In a large sauté pan over high heat, lightly brown butter. Add olive oil and diced pumpkin. Toss to coat and season with salt and pepper. Cook for about 2-3 minutes or until lightly caramelized. Add honey, toss to distribute, and cook 30 seconds (be careful not to let it get it too dark). Add vinegar and toss to deglaze. Check seasoning and adjust if necessary. Set aside.

To prepare the pumpkin seeds:

Preheat oven to 375°F.

Place pumpkin seeds in an oven-safe pan and lightly coat with oil. Season with salt and pepper. Roast in the oven for 3-6 minutes, until lightly toasted and fragrant. Set aside.

SANFORD RESTAURANT

For the soup:

¼ cup butter

1 pound onion, medium dice

¼ teaspoon cinnamon

½ teaspoon nutmeg

¼ teaspoon red chili flakes

1½ cups white wine

2 bay leaves

4 sprigs thyme

1 stick cinnamon

3¼ cups vegetable or chicken stock

roasted pumpkin

salt and pepper, to taste

To prepare the soup:

In a pot over medium heat, brown butter to a deep golden brown. Add onion and cook for 3–5 minutes (or until translucent or tender). Add ground cinnamon, nutmeg, and red chili flakes and cook 2–3 minutes, until toasted and aromatic. Add white wine, bay leaves, thyme, and cinnamon stick, and reduce by two-thirds, or until about a ½ cup of liquid is left. Add stock and roasted pumpkin. Bring to a gentle boil and simmer for a few minutes to soften and incorporate pumpkin all the way through. Puree in a blender and pass through a medium strainer. Adjust seasoning to taste with salt and pepper.

To serve, place soup in bowls and garnish with a few pumpkin seeds and caramelized pumpkin.

Brightonwoods Orchard

Burlington, Wisconsin
brightonwoodsorchard.com

William Stone married into the apple business. He found himself enamored of the science and art of orchardry after assuming care of his father-in-law, Irving Puntenney's, orchard in 1980.

At the time, the orchard consisted of about twenty-five varieties of heirloom apples, which Puntenney had planted on three acres of farmland he'd purchased in 1950 in Burlington, Wisconsin. Growing apples was a hobby; he grew varieties he'd enjoyed while growing up on a farm in Illinois. He'd harvest them and sell them by the bushel under an old bur oak tree on the property.

Stone, a medical oncologist by trade, also took up the orchard as a hobby. But by the mid-1980s, he'd taken a grafting course and began building the collection of apple trees that currently exist at Brightonwoods Orchard, a family business he operates with his wife, Judith, and her sister, Paula Puntenney.

After he began educating himself in the art of orchardry, Stone decided to plant over a thousand semi-dwarf trees and transition the orchard to accommodate the more modern method of high-density apple growing. In high-density growing, the trees are kept shorter, allowing them to make better use of photosynthetic energy. They produce less fruit than traditional trees (one and a half to three bushels per semi-dwarf tree in comparison to twenty bushels from a twenty foot traditionally grown tree), but the quality of fruit is vastly improved.

In 1997, Bill retired from oncology at the age of fifty-five. He was still young enough to handle the physical labor required to maintain the orchard, so he decided to expand. He began grafting onto smaller and smaller roots, creating dwarf trees. In response, he says, the spacing between the fruit trees had to be adjusted and trellises needed to be implemented to support them. Reduced yearly rainfall combined with

the dwarf trees' smaller, shallower roots meant that irrigation had to be installed. But these were trade-offs well worth the effort.

Four years later, they were at a crossroads. If they wanted to continue with the orchard, it needed to be profitable. So they chose to add a farm store where they could sell their fruit, establish an apple cider facility, and begin selling their apples at off-premise markets. Around the same time, they partnered with Charles and Milissa McGonegal, who established the now renowned Aeppeltreow Winery & Distillery on the property.

Today, Brightonwoods Orchard grows about seven hundred trees per acre with production of over a thousand bushels per year using integrated pest management. They grow about two hundred types of apples, including both new cultivars and heirloom apples that hail from countries such as Germany, Canada, France, Russia, and New Zealand. They also grow about twenty varieties of pears, along with a small amount of quince. Thanks to the establishment of the farm store and cidery, they sell 70 percent of their apple products on-site.

In addition to consumer sales, Brightonwoods works with a handful of restaurants. Dave Swanson of Braise was among the orchard's first customers. He began purchasing their apples for his Braise RSA and eventually hosted annual farm dinners at the orchard. Other chefs followed, including Peter Sandroni of La Merenda and Engine Company No. 3 in Milwaukee; Andrew Schneider from Le Rêve in Wauwatosa; and Mary Acuna, founder and co-owner of The Red Oak in Bristol. The orchard has also supplied fruit to Justin Aprahamian of Sanford in Milwaukee, who has often purchased their entire crop of quince.

Thyme-Roasted Apple Tart with Apple Salad

Chef Andrew Schneider, Le Rêve Patisserie & Café with apples from Brightonwoods Orchard

Chef Andrew Schneider has had a relationship with Bill Stone and the family at Brightonwoods for years. Their cider made him realize how superior local cider is to store-bought, and the quality of their apples made him commit to sourcing from them for the restaurant. Sourcing locally saved the restaurant during the COVID-19 pandemic, since they could just drive to local farms to pick up ingredients as needed rather than relying on distributors.

This apple tart mixes sweet and savory elements in a memorable autumnal starter that's comforting, yet fresh and bright.

SERVES 4

For the tart:

- 1 sheet puff pastry, thawed (or make from scratch if you're feeling ambitious)
- 4 orchard apples, cored and cut into thick slices (Bill at Brightonwoods recommends Williams Pride and Smokehouse varieties for roasting)
- 2 ounces unsalted Wisconsin butter
- 2 sprigs fresh thyme
- kosher salt
- freshly ground black pepper
- 3–4 ounces fresh LaClare Farms chèvre
- 6 ounces pecans, either roasted and salted or lightly smoked
- extra virgin olive oil

To prepare the tart:

Preheat the oven to 375°F.

Open thawed puff pastry and, using a fork, dock or poke scattered holes, maybe ten fork holes throughout the dough. The holes will allow steam to escape and the dough to rise consistently. Line a cookie sheet with parchment paper and place dough onto the pan. Repeat with another piece of parchment over the dough and a second cookie sheet on top of the dough. Place in oven and bake for 20–25 minutes or until dough is cooked and golden brown. An internal temperature of 200°F in the center ensures that it is fully baked. Remove from oven, carefully removing the top pan and setting aside to cool.

Core and cut apples into thick slices and place them in an oven-safe pan with butter, fresh thyme, salt, and pepper. Roast in the oven for 10 minutes and remove to cool at room temperature.

To build the tart, sprinkle the baked dough with cheese, roasted apples, and pecans. Lightly drizzle with extra virgin olive oil and warm in the oven for 5–8 minutes until cheese melts.

For the apple cider vinaigrette:

½ cup apple cider

½ cup extra virgin olive oil

2 tablespoons apple cider vinegar

For the apple salad:

1–2 orchard apples, cored and sliced

1 fennel bulb, shaved

1 blood orange, supremed

farmers market greens

To prepare the salad:

Whisk together vinaigrette ingredients and toss with sliced apples, shaved fennel, blood orange segments, and greens in a large bowl.

Serve slices of the apple tart with a portion of apple salad on the side.

LarryVille Gardens

Burlington, Wisconsin
larryvillegardens.com

It was a fateful day in 2018 when Michelle Cannon, a Burlington police officer, issued a ticket to a local resident. As they talked, the woman mentioned that she was starting a local farmers market.

The interaction gave Michelle pause. Maybe, she thought, it would be nice to grow food and sell it at the farmers market. If nothing else, it would be a far more pleasant pastime than giving out tickets, so she decided to apply for a position at the market.

Michelle and her husband, Larry, had lived on an eleven-and-a-half-acre property for twenty years. For many of those years, she lent it to a local farmer. But as she realized the extent to which commercial farming had robbed the land of its nutrients, she decided to bring it back. She took the parcel of fertilizer-fatigued earth and began the renewal process, adding manure and compost to the depleted soil. Then she began to grow vegetables.

At first, the couple just grew things for themselves. But when Michelle fell in love with the people she met at the farmers market, the notion of healing her soil and producing flavorful, nutrient-dense vegetables made her excited about taking on farming in a larger way. She named her farm for her husband, a recent retiree who had been spending more time at the farm.

As the business grew and farm work began to outpace what she could accomplish on her own, she solicited help from Morgan Sisson, who assisted her in starting the Worker Bees, a volunteer-based program that offers participants a vegetable share in exchange for working on the farm for a few hours a week during the growing season.

Over time, she also added a revenue stream to her business by building a small barn on her property and transforming it into The Source, a farm store where customers can purchase farm-fresh vegetables along with local dairy products, poultry, beef, pork, and a variety of artisan products.

Today, Michelle operates a Certified Naturally Grown farm where she grows vegetables year-round with help from both a greenhouse and a high tunnel. She starts her plants from seed and grows vegetables that she wants to eat, including heirloom tomatoes, Duganski garlic, summer leeks, head lettuce, fresh herbs, and winter spinach. She also grows a variety of vegetables that store well, including dried beans and potatoes.

When the COVID-19 pandemic hit and Michelle lost access to customers at the farmers market, she shifted her business model and began working more closely with restaurants. The decision was a sound financial move, but one that definitely posed a learning curve. Ultimately, she chose to hand-pick the restaurants she works with, ensuring that her relationships with chefs and eateries are built on mutual respect and admiration. Among her customers, she notes that Red Oak Restaurant has been a fabulous partner that showcases LarryVille Gardens' vegetables regularly on their menu.

In reflecting on her work, Michelle says she continues to take inspiration from the process of rejuvenating and regenerating the soil. It's a task that has given her something new to work toward every day and which she hopes will leave a healthier, more sustainable legacy for her grandchildren.

Beet and Kale Salad

Red Oak Restaurant
with vegetables from LarryVille Gardens

At Red Oak, they pride themselves in showcasing as many Wisconsin producers as possible. The star of this simple salad is LarryVille Gardens' red and gold baby beets and kale. But it also includes V&K honey, BelGioioso Gran Parma parmesan, and Wilson Farm Meats bacon. Farm-fresh produce is the big secret behind the flavor.

SERVES 4

For the roasted beets:

1 pound baby beets, cleaned and leaves and stems removed

2½ cups non-GMO rice bran oil

pinch of kosher salt

2 tablespoons V&K honey or preferred honey

For the vinaigrette:

1 tablespoon garlic, crushed

1 lemon, juiced and zested

1 shallot, finely diced

1 tablespoon white wine vinegar

¾ cup extra virgin olive oil

For the salad:

8 ounces baby kale, washed

roasted beets

2 ounces Parmesan, shaved

2 ounces pine nuts, toasted

3 ounces cooked bacon, chopped

To prepare the beets:

Preheat the oven to 350°F.

Add the beets and rice oil to an oven-safe pan, tossing the beets until they are fully coated with oil. Add a pinch of kosher salt and stir to combine. Then cover the pan and place it in the preheated oven, pulling the pan out after 35 minutes and shaking it to ensure that the beets don't stick to the bottom. Bake for 1 hour or until the beet skin can easily be peeled off with a clean kitchen towel. When the beets are fully cooked, uncover and allow them to sit for at least 5 minutes. While the beets are still warm, peel the skin with a clean kitchen towel that you don't mind staining with beet juices. After all the beets are peeled, cut them into fourths, place them into a medium bowl, and mix them with honey to coat. Chill the honey-coated beets in the refrigerator.

To prepare the lemon vinaigrette:

Place all ingredients except the olive oil into a mixing bowl and whisk together. While still whisking slowly, drizzle the olive oil into the vinaigrette until emulsified. If you prefer, you can make the vinaigrette in a food processor, following the same steps.

To prepare the salad:

Chop the kale roughly the same size as the quartered beets. Place the kale, roasted beets, Parmesan, pine nuts, and bacon into a large mixing bowl. Add about half of the vinaigrette and toss thoroughly. Taste, adding more vinaigrette as needed.

Lone Duck Farm

West Bend, Wisconsin
loneduckfarm.com

In 2008, Matt and Elise Susnik attended a presentation by Will Allen, the founder of Milwaukee's Growing Power. The presentation covered the urban farm's operations, including composting, soil reclamation, aquaculture, and aquaponics. But it was the aquaponics that piqued their interest.

After a decade of work in engineering, Matt Susnik decided he needed a break from the corporate world. He and Elise had always gardened, he had kept fish tanks and enjoyed fishing, and, thanks to membership in a local community-supported agriculture (CSA) program, he'd also developed an interest in the world of local food.

Aquaponics—a synergistic ecosystem in which fish produce nutrients for plants and the plants clean the water for the fish—was appealing in terms of its efficient use of space and because it produces both protein and greens. The Susniks were also drawn to aquaponics because it meant they could grow a significant amount of produce on their small five-acre lot without having to clear the land of trees. So Matt did the research, and in fall of 2010 he built a 30 × 70 foot greenhouse in which he began growing lettuce and eventually up to thirty types of greens.

Business grew quickly. Lone Duck Farm sold largely through the farmers market for the first two years. They also launched a CSA for their fresh greens. By the end of the first year, the farm was working with Chef Jodi Kanzenbach of Cafe Soeurette, a farm-to-table restaurant in West Bend, who helped them get their feet wet in the restaurant sphere. By year two, they'd also started working with Chef Cole Ersel at Wolf Peach, with whom they'd sit down and plan what to grow on the basis of what he needed for the restaurant menu.

LONE DUCK FARM

Each year, business grew. Restaurants like Goodkind and Morel in Milwaukee along with Trattoria Stefano in Sheboygan became loyal customers, so much so that by the time Wolf Peach closed in 2018, Lone Duck had enough restaurant business that others could make up the difference.

After a time, Lone Duck's crops were shaped by the chefs, who would request items they couldn't find elsewhere on the market. For example, Chef Dane Baldwin of The Diplomat in Milwaukee had a standing order for a unique heirloom baby purple romaine. Beyond being delicious, the greens made an eye-catching statement on the plate.

Prior to the start of the COVID-19 pandemic in 2020, nearly 90 percent of the farm's sales were from restaurants. As restaurants shuttered and sales fell off, Matt says a kind post about Lone Duck's greens posted by Odd Duck on Instagram gave the farm a notable boost in consumer sales. Their CSA membership grew, and the new business filled the gaps that had been left by restaurants. The farm was again operating at full capacity, producing over forty thousand heads of lettuce, plus pak choy, microgreens, and a variety of shoots every year.

Today, Matt continues to consider his options and looks for creative and new ways to serve his customers. Every day presents a new challenge, and Lone Duck is consistently evolving to serve an ever-changing local food scene.

Melon, Olive, and Goat Cheese Salad with Tarragon Vinaigrette

Colin Reigle, The Norbert
with greens from Lone Duck Farm

Who said a salad has to feature lettuce as its main ingredient? For Colin Reigle at The Norbert in West Bend, finding alternatives to the proverbial lettuce salad is always a welcome challenge. In this case, late summer melon shines alongside savory elements like olives and local goat cheese, while a fresh combination of herbs and baby lettuce from Lone Duck Farm pulls all the flavors together.

SERVES 4

For the tarragon vinaigrette:

1 tablespoon white wine vinegar

2 Meyer lemons, zested and juiced

6 sprigs of tarragon, leaves stripped, finely chopped

3 sprigs of thyme, leaves stripped, finely chopped

pinch of sugar

kosher salt and pepper, to taste

½ cup extra virgin olive oil

For the salad:

1 whole honeydew melon, seeded and cut into cubes or scooped with melon baller

1 whole cantaloupe, seeded and cut into cubes or scooped with melon baller

4 ounces goat cheese, crumbled

1 large shallot, thinly sliced

20 kalamata olives, pitted and halved

2–3 radishes, thinly sliced (the restaurant uses red, purple, and French breakfast radishes)

1 ounce toasted pepitas

fresh flat leaf parsley

fresh mint (use the sprouting, young leaves; if using larger leaves, rip them into pieces)

tarragon vinaigrette

For the garnish:

red veined sorrel

baby red oak lettuce

To prepare the vinaigrette:

Combine all ingredients except oil in a food processor. Blend until a uniform consistency is achieved. Slowly drizzle in oil until emulsified.

To prepare the salad:

Divide ingredients between four salad bowls or plates, arranging as desired. Use one tablespoon of vinaigrette per salad. Garnish with sorrel and baby red oak lettuce.

THE NORBERT

Hundred Acre

Milwaukee, Wisconsin
hundred-acre.org

Hundred Acre, an urban hydroponic farm located in the Century City business park, harvested its first crop of salad mix and Genovese basil on December 30, 2021. The harvest was donated to Feeding America as the kick-off for an ongoing partnership that supplies fresh food to families in need.

For Chris Corkery, a former chef and marketing professional who left his corporate career to pursue work that truly made a difference in the world, the inaugural harvest marked a huge milestone for the small start-up farm. But it was just the tip of the iceberg in terms of activating Hundred Acre's mission to leverage the power of fresh food, agricultural technologies, and light manufacturing to revitalize an underserved urban community and promote supply chain resilience. The farm could also be a catalyst that positioned the city as a leader in sustainable urban farming, building a model that could be reproduced in any city across the nation.

To accomplish its mission, the farm utilizes a five-thousand-square-foot controlled environmental system with vertical hydroponics, creating secure and traceable non-GMO produce, grown without pesticides or herbicides, which is available year-round and harvested weekly. Crops produced include a custom salad mix (composed of a blend of specialty hydroponic lettuces) and Genovese basil (a flavorful Italian varietal that grows well in a hydroponic environment).

In addition to growing food, the farm provides educational experiences in urban agriculture through field trips and seminars for high schools, universities, and other groups. Meanwhile, a partnership with the Milwaukee School of Engineering offers students a firsthand opportunity to study the business and apply their industrial engineering knowledge to the model as part of their senior projects. Workforce development and student apprenticeship programs are knit into the plans for Hundred Acre, with the aim of offering an educational pathway to local employment in the light industrial sector or food tech industry.

Hundred Acre currently sells to a few larger institutional buyers, including Sodexo USA and Midwest Foods, grocers including Sendik's, and a small network of local restaurants. Chefs have an open invitation to visit the farm and see how the salad mix and herbs are grown, but Chris also regularly delivers samples to their restaurants, allowing them to try out the vegetables and see how they fit into their menus. However, most of the chefs pick up any regular orders right at the growing facility.

For Hundred Acre, mutually beneficial relationships with local restaurants are key. The farm offers a consistent supply of produce in return for the financial support needed to sustain the farm and its mission. But restaurants also forge a vital connection between the farm and the larger community, providing an effective means for telling Hundred Acre's story.

Basil Panzanella

Chef Joe Muench, Buttermint Finer Dining & Cocktails
with Hundred Acre basil and mixed greens

First described in the 1500s in a poem by artist and poet Bronzino, panzanella salad has endured for centuries, providing a delicious way to bring new life to loaves of crusty bread that have passed their prime and making full use of beautifully juicy summer tomatoes. In this case, Chef Joe Muench has re-created a classic using fresh Milwaukee-grown Hundred Acre basil and mixed greens with fresh tomatoes, olives, and the rich, nutty flavor of LaClare Evalon, a raw goat's milk cheese made by LaClare Farms in Malone, Wisconsin.

This classic Italian panzanella is frugal, fresh, and seasonal, but still hearty enough to stand on its own as a fresh summer lunch or light supper.

SERVES 4 AS ENTRÉE-SIZE SALAD

For the vinaigrette:

1½ cups white balsamic vinegar
2 garlic cloves
2 tablespoons Dijon mustard
2 teaspoons Worcestershire sauce
8–10 anchovy fillets
1 tablespoon sugar, granulated
¾ cup extra virgin olive oil
kosher salt
black pepper

For the tomatoes and olives:

2 10-ounce packages of mixed sweet grape tomatoes
3 cups mixed whole olives: kalamata, picholine, arbequina, manzanilla
½ cup extra virgin olive oil
zest from one orange, peeled not grated
1 orange, juiced
2 fresh rosemary sprigs
2 fresh thyme sprigs
2 teaspoons black pepper

For the panzanella bread:

1 pound loaf of sturdy rustic bread (Italian country or sourdough is great), cut into 2-inch cubes (about 8 cups bread cubes)
½ cup water
¼ cup white balsamic vinegar
¼ cup olive oil
kosher salt
black pepper

For the farm egg:

½ cup extra virgin olive oil
4 eggs
kosher salt
black pepper

For the salad:

32 ounces mixed greens
4 ounces Genovese basil, stems removed
6–8 ounces LaClare Evalon cheese, shredded

STEPHEN FISHER/BLACK SHOE HOSPITALITY

To prepare the vinaigrette:

Place the vinegar, garlic, mustard, Worcestershire, anchovies, and sugar into the jar of a blender. Turn the blender on high and puree for 1–2 minutes. Turn the blender down to low and slowly pour in the olive oil. Taste for salt and pepper, adding as needed. This dressing can be prepared a couple days in advance and stored in a closed container in the refrigerator.

To prepare the tomatoes and olives:

Preheat the oven to 425°F.

Place all the ingredients into a bowl and toss to coat. Spread out on a parchment-lined sheet pan and place in the oven for 15 minutes. Stir the mixture every 5 minutes, roasting the tomatoes and olives until they are slightly blistered (about 20 minutes total). Pull from the oven and allow to cool to room temperature. Place in a small enough container so the mixture can keep marinating. This step can be done a day or two in advance. Store the tomato olive mix in a covered container in the refrigerator and bring to room temperature before adding to the salad.

To prepare the panzanella bread:

Place the bread in a bowl and lightly soak with water, adding more as needed. Squeeze the water out of the bread and discard the water. At this point, the bread should be soft and damp. Toss it with the olive oil and vinegar, and season with salt and pepper to taste. Set aside at room temperature.

To prepare the farm egg:

Heat a nonstick pan, big enough for four eggs, over medium heat. Add the olive oil to lightly coat the bottom. When the oil is shimmering, crack the eggs into the pan. For sunny-side up eggs, cook the eggs for 3–4 minutes. The edges should be starting to brown and the whites on top are almost cooked. Remove the eggs from the pan and place them on a parchment-lined sheet pan. Season each with salt and pepper. Keep at room temperature until you are ready to assemble the salads.

To assemble the salad:

Toss the greens with half the basil leaves and just over half of the vinaigrette, reserving the remainder of the vinaigrette for serving.

Layer half of the greens mixture on four serving plates. Randomly scatter some of the tomato and olive mixture as well as some of the bread on top of the greens, creating a first layer. Create a second layer of greens and the tomato olive mixture. Top the salads with the remaining basil leaves and the shredded Evalon cheese. Place one egg on top of each salad and finish with a few twists of freshly ground black pepper.

Serve salads with the remaining vinaigrette on the side.

Parkside 23 Farm

Brookfield, Wisconsin
parkside23.com

In Milwaukee, restaurants like Roots blazed the trail for farm-to-table dining in both the city and the surrounding area. Parkside 23, which opened almost a decade ago, followed solidly in those footsteps. However, they took the concept a step further by including a ten-thousand-square-foot farm in the plans for the property. And while the on-site farm is just one of many that fulfill the needs of the farm-to-table restaurant, it's become an integral part of its identity.

The farm, located just footsteps north of the restaurant, is maintained by resident farmer and edible landscaping professional John Harrigan,

who nurtures a collection of crops that range from summer squash and onions to peppers, Swiss chard, potatoes, raspberries, and herbs. John follows an agricultural approach that utilizes crop rotation, native plantings, and companion planting to minimize the need for chemicals.

Every spring, he sits down with the chef and restaurant staff to determine what to plant for the season. Throughout the season, John works in tandem with the restaurant staff to handle seasonal harvests. It's a relationship, John says, that has taught him a great deal about the use of produce in a restaurant kitchen, as well as giving him the opportunity to educate the chefs and staff about the farming process and seasonality.

During the growing season, farm-fresh produce becomes a feature at the restaurant, appearing in specials from Chef Michael Fifarek that highlight the best of the farm's seasonal produce. The farm is also the site for annual farm suppers, a tradition at the restaurant since its inception.

The intimate suppers, which include an educational tour with John and a meal featuring produce from the farm, are offered during four-day stretches throughout the growing season during the months of July, August, and September, giving guests an opportunity to experience meals that reflect the seasonal nature of produce in Wisconsin.

Beet Salad with Candied Maple Walnuts, Goat Cheese, and Cider Vinaigrette

Chef Michael Fifarek, Parkside 23
With beets from the Parkside 23 Farm

The menu at Parkside 23 is inspired largely by the vegetables harvested from the farm. In this recipe, fresh beets are roasted to bring out their sweetness and then combined with candied walnuts, fresh goat cheese, and a simple apple cider vinaigrette. The salad originally began as an early autumn special, but it has since become a staple on the menu due to its popularity with guests.

Note: You'll likely have some leftover vinaigrette. It will keep in the refrigerator for up to two weeks stored in an airtight container.

SERVES 6 AS STARTER SALAD

For the salad:

3 large red beets, washed and trimmed

3 large gold beets, washed and trimmed

4 ounces arugula

4 ounces fresh goat cheese, crumbled

For maple coated walnuts:

2 tablespoons unsalted butter

⅓ cup maple syrup

8 ounces walnuts

1 teaspoon salt

To prepare the beets:

Preheat the oven to 325°F.

Wrap beets in aluminum foil (keep red and gold beets separate) and bake in a preheated oven for about two hours (total time needed will depend on both the size of the beets and their color; the gold beets tend to finish before the red). When beets are done, a knife should penetrate them with little resistance. Allow beets to cool (they can be prepared a day ahead), and then peel and dice into bite-size squares.

To prepare the walnuts:

Preheat the oven to 350°F.

In a small saucepan, melt butter and maple syrup together over medium heat. Place walnuts in a small bowl, pour maple syrup mixture over them, sprinkle with salt, and mix well. Spread the coated walnuts on a baking sheet and bake in a preheated oven for 6 minutes, checking and stirring frequently. Remove walnuts from the oven and place them on a wire screen or fine gauge cooling rack set on top of another baking sheet, spreading them out evenly. Place walnuts back into the oven to dry roast for another 4–6 minutes, watching them carefully so they do not burn. Remove from the oven and allow to cool.

LORI FREDRICH

PARKSIDE
TWENTY THREE

For the apple cider vinaigrette:

2 Granny Smith apples, peeled, cored, and diced

¼ cup apple cider vinegar

1 tablespoon sugar

1 teaspoon salt

zest of 1 lemon

½ teaspoon vanilla extract

1 cup canola oil

To prepare apple cider vinaigrette:

Combine all the ingredients, except the canola oil, in a blender and puree until smooth. Very slowly drizzle canola oil into the running blender and blend until emulsified.

To compose the salad:

Place the two types of beets and arugula in separate medium bowls. Coat each lightly with dressing and toss gently to mix. Set aside a small amount of the arugula for garnish; then divide the remaining arugula among 6 single-serving plates. Follow with a layer of golden beets, a layer of red beets, and crumbled goat cheese. Divide the walnuts between the plates. Garnish each plate with a bit more of the reserved arugula.

Summer Squash Salad

Chef Jonathan Manyo, Morel
with squash from Amy's Acre

This simple summer dish is easy to prepare on a hot day, and it makes the perfect starter. Heat from the chili is balanced by the saltiness of the feta and the cooling effect of mint while everything is balanced by a pop of acid from the lemon. This recipe can be easily doubled or tripled for a larger group.

SERVES 6

2 green zucchini squash

2 yellow zucchini or crookneck squash

6 ounces crumbled feta cheese

¼ cup pine nuts

12 mint leaves, chiffonade (sliced very thin)

¼ teaspoon red chili flakes, toasted

1 lemon, juiced

¼ cup extra virgin olive oil

kosher salt and pepper, to taste

MIC KELLOGG MOREL

Wash and dry the squash. Slice the squash very thin into long ribbons, using a mandolin or vegetable peeler, and place in a bowl large enough to toss. Add the feta, pine nuts, mint, and chili flakes. In a separate bowl, mix the lemon juice and olive oil. When ready to serve, season the squash mixture with salt and pepper and add the lemon/oil mixture. Toss everything together and serve.

Cattail Organics

Athens, Wisconsin
cattailorganics.com

Kat Becker grew up in the Morningside Heights neighborhood in New York City, far from the areas in Upstate New York where farm-fresh produce was grown. But when she entered high school, her interest in volunteerism drew her to work for mobile food pantries and prepared meal programs in the city, both of which contributed to a strong interest in food justice and an awareness of the complexity of the food system. When she reached college age, she enrolled at Cornell University with the goal of studying food policy. While there, her interest in agriculture grew, so she decided to pursue graduate work at the University of Wisconsin–Madison, where the passionate local food movement and the world of community-supported agriculture appealed to her.

In 2006, she married her first husband and started her first community-supported agriculture (CSA) farm on his parents' land. At that point, the local food movement in the area surrounding Wausau, Wisconsin, was still developing, so Kat poured herself into the work of educating people about local food. She also became the face of the farm in terms of wholesale relationships.

Unfortunately, her marriage didn't fare as well as her farm. In 2016, she left to branch off on her own. Her mother, who had moved to the area to be closer to family in 2012, had purchased property nearby. Kat bought her mother's home and the fifty acres of land that surrounded it. Her former husband retained both the CSA and the brand, but she retained the farm's wholesale clients, betting on her ability to recoup her farm sales by leveraging the strength of their preexisting business.

As she built the new farm, she rejected many of the systems that hadn't been efficient on the former farm. She maintained a focus on organic methods but concentrated on growing varieties of vegetables that have been created for both their superior flavor and their performance, including specialty salad mix and a variety of carrots. At the same time, she decided to focus on selling pristine produce that was nicely packaged and clearly branded.

The approach worked. Her business turned a profit in a relatively short period of time, and she found that all of her customers—from chefs and grocers to CSA and market customers—appreciated the high quality, cleanliness, and packaging of the produce she delivered. By 2019, Kat had rebuilt her business. She'd also gotten remarried to Logan Brock, another

local farmer who operates Growing Earth Farm. Today the two work side by side, each maintaining their own successful brands.

Today, Cattail Organics focuses on offering chefs a slate of seasonal vegetables at their peak of freshness. Twice a year (in the fall and after the new year), Kat communicates with her wholesale accounts to determine what worked and what didn't, adjusting her procedures accordingly for the next season.

Her approach to restaurants has been largely about getting to know the chefs, what they like to use, and how much they will typically buy. On occasion, she'll take on special requests from chefs for unique produce or particular items they need. But she says keeping communication open about needs and budgets is also important, especially for accounts like Red Eye Brewing Company, which tends to purchase in volume.

Kat says she's attracted to the challenges of organic farming, which often requires constant change, but the reward is producing vegetables that are truly delicious and deliver on both flavor and high nutrient levels. She's also very proud that she's been able to contribute to a wide variety of programs that impact the food system at large, including assisting the Marathon County Hunger Coalition with a food bank CSA program during the pandemic, working the local farm to schools program, and mentoring other local farmers.

Roasted Beet Salad with Truffled Goat Cheese and Red Wine Gastrique

Chef Nathan Bychinski, Red Eye Brewing Company
with vegetables from Cattail Organics

Traditional beet and goat cheese salad gets an upgrade in this fresh take from Chef Nathan Bychinski featuring farm-fresh vegetables, plenty of fresh herbs, a flavorful red wine gastrique, and pumpernickel croutons. A garnish of tart sorrel leaves adds a balancing punch.

SERVES 4

For the truffled goat cheese:

1 cup goat cheese, room temperature

1–2 tablespoons truffle oil

zest of 1 lemon

kosher salt and pepper, to taste

For the beets:

6 beets (Chioggia and golden)

2–3 tablespoons kosher salt

olive oil, to coat

2–3 tablespoons red wine vinegar

kosher salt, to taste

3 sprigs of thyme

8 garlic cloves

black pepper

For the red wine gastrique:

½ cup red wine vinegar

1 spring of thyme

2 garlic cloves

5 peppercorns

1 bay leaf

2 tablespoons sugar

1 tablespoon kosher salt

1–2 teaspoon guar gum

To prepare the truffled goat cheese:

Place ingredients into a mixing bowl. Mix thoroughly, and check seasoning. Set aside until ready to serve.

To prepare the beets:

Preheat the oven to 400°F.

Wash beets and cut tops off. Spread salt evenly in a small roasting pan, and place the cut ends of the beets on the salt. Coat the beets with olive oil and season with vinegar and salt. Place aromatics in the pan and cover with aluminum foil. Roast in the oven for about 1 hour or until a knife can easily pierce the beets. Let the beets cool down for about 30 minutes; peel while still warm. Cut beets into quarters or smaller depending on the size of the beets. Place in the refrigerator until completely cooled.

To prepare the red wine gastrique:

Place all ingredients in a small saucepan except guar gum. Bring to a boil and simmer for 10 minutes. Turn off heat and steep for 20–30 minutes. Strain and cool; whisk in guar gum to thicken gastrique. Reserve for later.

For the pumpernickel croutons:

4 slices pumpernickel bread,
  ¼-inch cubes

3 tablespoons butter, melted

kosher salt, to taste

For the garnish:

Maldon sea salt

olive oil

½ cup sorrel leaves

¼ cup toasted hazelnuts, chopped

To prepare the croutons:

Preheat the oven to 350°F.

Toss bread cubes with melted butter and salt. Bake in the oven for 10–15 minutes or until toasted.

To plate the salad:

Spread goat cheese on plates evenly. Place beet pieces in a small pan and brush with gastrique. Arrange beets on top of goat cheese, and season with Maldon salt and olive oil. To finish, top with pumpernickel croutons, sorrel, and hazelnuts.

Farm Happy

Jackson, Wisconsin
farmhappyjackson.com

John McConville had spent years as a professional whitewater kayaker, a profession that required him to give 110 percent. When he gave it all up to return home and help his family, he had no idea that the turn his career would take would be just as challenging.

It began with a small garden in his parents' backyard, where John began growing vegetables to feed the family. As his interest in gardening grew, he began to seek out opportunities to learn even more. In 2015, he met Jennifer Gordon, an avid gardener who had years of experience

FARM HAPPY

volunteering at local farms and working in hydroponics and beekeeping. Drawn together by a common passion, the two began gardening together, transforming ten acres of former horse-pasture land into a small-but-efficient vegetable farm they named Farm Happy.

Today, John and Jennifer intensely farm about two acres of their ten-acre tract of land, extending the season for crops like greens and carrots with the use of caterpillar tunnels and using greenhouses and trellising to ward off disease in crops like tomatoes. They also make use of techniques like crop rotation, composting, and cover crops to renew the energy in the soil, providing a fertile landscape for their vegetable crops, which include microgreens, lettuce, spinach, and at least twenty to thirty unusual varieties of tomatoes in shapes and colors that vary from yellow to green and purple.

The two started their business selling vegetables at the farmers market. At one of their first markets, a chef approached their stand and asked whether they could grow things like Mexican sour gherkins. The conversation inspired them to think about the types of crops they might grow in the future, but it also inspired them to continue showing up each week, ultimately earning the trust of both consumers and chefs.

That trust has earned Farm Happy a core of restaurant customers—including Odd Duck, Belfrē Kitchen, and I.d. in Delafield—on which they can rely not only for regular orders but also to assist them in clearing out inventory when they have a larger than average harvest of vegetables. Their work with restaurants, which represents up to 70 percent of their income, has assisted them in growing their business, and it's given them a great deal of pride to see their produce make it onto the plate in some of the area's most prominent restaurants.

Every day, John says he's amazed by nature: from the process of taking a seed, planting it in February, and raising a sixteen-foot plant by the end of October to simply watching the daily life cycle on the farm, tasting the fruits of the land, and making the connection between the food and the soil. He and Jennifer understand and appreciate how much all the hard work they put into their farm is returned to them in spades as they harvest their seasonal delicacies and watch them being put to great use.

Coffee-Seasoned Carrots with Spiced Yogurt

Chef Thi Cao, Wild Roots
with carrots from Farm Happy

Chef Thi Cao says that he's grown to trust the expertise of the farmers with whom he works, counting on them to know what they grow best and what is fresh. He bases his ever-changing menu on their list of what's fresh and in season.

When carrots at Farm Happy come up on the fresh list, he works to incorporate them into his menu, often adding unexpected elements to pique guests' interest. In this case, a bit of bitterness from locally roasted coffee offsets the natural sweetness of the carrots, and the accompanying spiced yogurt offers a pop of freshness and acidity to balance the dish.

This recipe can be easily doubled or tripled if you are feeding more than four people. Just be sure to adjust the size of your pan accordingly.

SERVES 4

For the spiced yogurt:

1 cup plain yogurt

1 tablespoon chopped fresh chives

1 tablespoon chopped fresh parsley

⅛ teaspoon cayenne pepper

⅛ teaspoon cumin

½ tablespoon lemon juice

For the carrots:

1 pound fresh unpeeled baby rainbow carrots

2 tablespoons unsalted butter

1 tablespoon granulated sugar

kosher salt, to taste

fresh finely ground coffee, to taste (Thi uses Valentine Coffee)

To prepare the spiced yogurt:

Whisk together yogurt, chives, parsley, cayenne pepper, cumin, and lemon juice until well combined. Set aside until you are ready to serve. Yogurt sauce can be made ahead; store for up to 24 hours in a sealed container in the refrigerator.

To prepare the carrots:

If using rainbow carrots, do not peel the skins. Trim the green tops down to nubs, and then wash and dry thoroughly.

Melt butter in a sauté pan over medium heat. Add sugar into the pan, and then add the carrots. Toss the carrots until completely coated and cook until fork tender. Depending on the size of the carrots, it may take 6–9 minutes for the carrots to become tender.

Season with salt and a few pinches of ground coffee to taste. Serve immediately with spiced yogurt.

Bacon-Braised Cabbage

Chef Daniel Fox, Heritage Tavern

Chef Daniel Fox's interpretation of this classic German dish is lovely served with his recipes for Mushroom and Swiss Bratwurst and Sour Cream Spaetzle (see pages 162 and 96). But it's a worthy side dish that complements any number of braised meats or pierogi.

SERVES 4-6

For the braised cabbage:

3 ounces bacon ends, diced small (high-quality sliced bacon can also be used)

1 red onion, julienned

4 garlic cloves, minced

1 head purple cabbage, cut into quarters, core removed, julienned (food processor works well)

1 tablespoon kosher salt

6 ounces red wine vinegar

3 ounces dry red wine

For the bouquet garni:

Place the following herbs and spices in a small cheesecloth bag or tea infuser:

1 teaspoon juniper

1 teaspoon coriander

1 teaspoon whole peppercorns

1 bay leaf

1-2 sprigs fresh thyme

Preheat the oven to 350°F.

On the stovetop, heat a Dutch oven over medium-high heat. Render the bacon until cooked partway through, and then add onions and garlic to sweat. Do not let them color. Add the cabbage as well as the salt to help it break down. Sweat the cabbage until it loosens up (a few minutes).

Deglaze the pot with the red wine vinegar and red wine, and add the bouquet garni. Put the lid on the Dutch oven and place it in the oven for about 20 minutes.

After 20 minutes, take a look at how much liquid remains in the pan. If there is a significant amount, return the pot to the oven and allow it to cook until it reduces and becomes like a glaze. Serve warm.

Braised cabbage will hold for days if kept in an airtight container in the refrigerator. Reheat before serving.

PAULIUS MUSTEIKIS

Ukwakhwa (Our Foods)

Oneida Reservation, Wisconsin
ukwakhwa.com

White corn has been an integral part of the ancestry of the Oneida people for over two thousand years. Considered the oldest of the Three Sisters, white corn formed a sacred foundation of the Oneida diet along-side its sisters, beans and squash. Even as their nation was divided by colonization, the connection to corn—along with much of their cultural heritage—was retained by a handful of families, ensuring that it would not be lost to history.

Thanks in part to the food sovereignty movement that's taking place across the country, the Oneida Nation is among many indigenous groups reclaiming their right to sustainably produced, culturally appropriate food and traditional agricultural systems.

Rebecca Webster is at the helm of one such movement, which takes the form of Ukwakhwa (Our Foods), a ten-acre farm and 501(c)(3) nonprofit. Ukwakhwa produces heirloom, indigenous foods while facilitating seed saving and educational programming. Their philosophy is that every time an indigenous person plants a seed, it is an act of resistance, an assertion of sovereignty, and a reclamation of identity.

Rebecca and her husband, Steve, both grew up on the reservation in Christian families. Growing up, neither were allowed to participate in traditional Oneida ceremonies, and Rebecca says her family bussed her to a public school off the reservation rather than allow her to attend the tribal school. As a result, most of what she knew about her culture she gleaned from books. For years, much of her culture remained a mystery. However, as she neared adulthood, attitudes on the reservation began to change, and her family started to reconnect to their culture through both their native language and their food.

When Rebecca and Steve got married, they made it a point to garden, growing a variety of indigenous foods, including the Three Sisters. As they cultivated their ancestral foods, they learned the traditional names, the stories, and the manner in which they were used, as both food and medicine. They also began forging connections with others, including members of the extended Haudenosaunee community in New York, where the Oneida Nation originally resided before being moved to the reservation in Wisconsin.

In 2017, Rebecca and Steve purchased ten acres of land on the Oneida Reservation, built a home, and began growing a variety of Haudenosaunee seeds, including corn, beans, squash, tobacco, sunflowers, sunchokes, elderberries, and strawberries. The farm uses a combination of traditional growing methods along with a high tunnel greenhouse to extend their growing season. In 2022, they also added a colony of bees to the farmstead.

Their intention was to assist the community in learning about their ancestral foods and reclaiming those foods and the agricultural heritage that came with them. While they don't produce enough volume on the farm to sell the produce, they do share their seeds with others who wish to start growing their own foods.

In 2021, Ukwakhwa achieved its 501(c)(3) nonprofit status, allowing it to apply for grants to fund educational programming about planting, growing, harvesting, seed saving, food preparation, and making traditional tools and crafts. Support for the project has allowed Rebecca and Steve to add a commercial kitchen space where they can hold cooking classes. Events, workshops, and farmstead tours are available on a sliding scale for corporations, government agencies, schools, and nonprofit organizations, making free and low-cost education available to organizations led by Black, Indigenous, and Latinx people.

Rebecca says the farmstead is just part of their journey to reclaim knowledge that was stolen, and she acknowledges that there is still much to learn. "We're reclaiming our foodways. In a time where we don't have to be ashamed of who we are, we are able to celebrate the relationships we have with our seed relatives. We're able to gather that information and

share it with both our local and extended communities. And there are enough of us that we are able to tell our stories on our own terms."

Rebecca has also written a book that traces the history of the Haudenosaunee's relationship with heirloom white corn, offering insights through the stories of fifty community members who cultivate the sacred ancestral food. *Our Precious Corn: Yukwanénste* will be published in 2023.

Oneida White Corn Mush

Chef Luke Zahm, Driftless Cafe
with white corn grown by the Oneida Nation

Chef Luke Zahm was first introduced to Ohe·lúku, an agricultural cooperative of Oneida Nation families growing native white corn, at Farm Aid in September of 2019. There he met Oneida tribal members Laura Manthe and Dr. Toni House, who sat down with him to tell the story of the sacred Oneida white corn and their efforts to

UKWAKHWA

revive her smoldering embers from the fire of their history. These women spoke with a passion and focus that seared into his soul and provided a storyline that he found simultaneously captivating, heartbreaking, and filled with hope for a better future. The experience also made Zahm realize that the story of the Oneida must be shared.

It doesn't take much research into the Oneida people to uncover the stories of removal from their homelands in Upstate New York and the tragedy that followed their people, their culture, and their food. But it is only recently that members of the Oneida Nation have begun to reconnect their stories to their culture through food. As Zahm learned through interviews with Rebecca Webster, Dr. Toni House, Laura Manthe, and Robin John, the Oneida people find their DNA in the stalks of their sacred white corn. It gives them a sense of connection, talks to them in the words of the Haudenosaunee "Peacemaker," and tells them they are doing the work of their ancestors.

This recipe is Chef Luke Zahm's adaptation of a traditional method of cooking the Oneida white corn with maple syrup in the form of "mush." It was created to honor the Oneida (and all indigenous people everywhere). For that reason, Luke specifies that it must be cooked with respect, without symbols of colonization (no dairy), and with a heart open to hearing the stories of the people who have lived to bring us both the corn and her proud heritage.

SERVES 6-8

1 cup whole dried Oneida white corn*

6 cups organic stock or water

1½ tablespoons kosher salt

1 teaspoon white pepper

2 tablespoons white miso

maple syrup to drizzle (optional)

*White corn is available for purchase at the Oneida One Stop convenience stores located within the Oneida Reservation near Green Bay, Wisconsin.

Using a spice mill or food grinder, finely grind 1 cup of whole kernel dried white corn. One cup of kernels will yield about 2 cups of ground corn.

Place the ground corn in a pot large enough to accommodate 6 cups of liquid, plus room for stirring. Add 6 cups of cold stock or water to the corn and allow it to sit for at least 45 minutes, or as long as overnight, to rehydrate the corn (the longer the corn is allowed to sit cold, the shorter the cooking time will be).

Once rehydrated, bring the corn and liquid to a simmer, and add 1½ tablespoons of kosher salt and 1 teaspoon of white pepper. Stir constantly to prevent scorching. Once the corn is tender and thickened, add 2 tablespoons of white miso and stir to incorporate. Remove from heat and allow to rest.

Serve as a main course or as a side with grilled meat or mushrooms. Mush can also be served with maple syrup.

Sour Cream Spaetzle

Chef Daniel Fox, Heritage Tavern

Chef Daniel Fox's recipe for traditional German dumplings is the perfect accompa-
niment for his Mushroom and Swiss Bratwurst and his Bacon-Braised Cabbage (see
pages 162 and 90). But this versatile recipe can be enjoyed many ways, including
alongside braised meats, stews, or as a (very nontraditional) alternative to gnocchi.

SERVES 4-6

1¾ cup all-purpose
flour

2 teaspoon kosher salt

1½ cup sour cream

dash of sriracha

2 eggs

canola oil, enough to
prevent sticking

1–2 tablespoons butter,
to finish

Whisk together the flour and salt until combined. In a stand mixer with the paddle attachment, combine the sour cream, sriracha, and eggs. Add the flour mixture and whip it all together for several minutes. The batter should have an elastic consistency.

Prepare a lightly oiled tray or sheet pan and bring a large pot of water to a boil. If you have a traditional spaetzle maker, work in batches. Set up the spaetzle maker over the boiling water, fill it with some of the dough, and slide it back and forth. The dumplings will cook for about 45 seconds. Once the water comes back up to a boil, stir them around, and give them about 20 seconds.

When the spaetzles have risen to the top of the water, they're done. Put them on a tray and drizzle a little canola oil over them, and then let them cool. These can be made a day ahead. Just store them in an airtight container in the refrigerator. When you're ready to finish them, heat a small nonstick pan over medium-high heat. Drop the spaetzles into the pan and sear them off. Once they have a little color, add a dollop of butter to finish.

Bower's Produce

East Troy, Wisconsin
facebook.com/bowersproduce

It was 1960 when Robert and Shirley Bower began farming on thirty-two acres of land in East Troy. Over the years, the farm grew, eventually occupying seventy acres, where all nine of their children spent time working while they were growing up.

For years, Bower's did well supplying vegetables to local grocers, but as national distribution channels grew more common, they found themselves looking for other revenue streams. In the 1970s, they established a roadside stand on the property, which became a haven for locals to purchase farm-fresh produce.

In time, ownership of the land was passed to the Bower children. But it was Chuck Bower who felt the spirit of the soil in his blood and kept the farm operating, even after his parents passed away. His love for soil science and his passion for the land drive his approach to farming, using low-till methods to maintain and enhance the biological integrity of the soil while also promoting water conservation and eschewing chemicals in favor of more natural methods.

Chuck's brother Mert, who had moved away from the farm in 1982, recently moved back to East Troy with his wife, Laura, and built a home on his family's land. Laura assists in running the farm's roadside stand, and Mert says he looks forward to supporting his brother's passion and work on the family farm.

In addition to fields of vegetables and an apple orchard, Bower's Produce operates fourteen greenhouses, which are used for seeding crops and establishing bedding plants to sell. Chuck's partner, Maria, has also begun growing flowers, which are sold alongside the produce at Bower's farm stand as well as at the West Allis Farmers Market.

While the farm doesn't currently solicit business from area restaurants, the markets where Bower's sells are a draw for local chefs. At least a dozen of them, including Scott Whalen of Belfrē Kitchen, drop by on a weekly basis to check what's in season and purchase bundles of fresh produce for their restaurants.

Head to the market in early spring, and you'll find plenty of flowers, hanging baskets, and bedding plants for sale. But as the growing season takes hold, the market fills with sweet corn, tomatoes, peppers, and melons, along with a variety of other produce. By autumn, the farm's orchards produce a wide variety of apples, which are sold along with pumpkins and winter squash.

BELFRĒ KITCHEN

Roasted Brussels Sprouts with Chestnut Apple Coulis

Sous Chef Scott Whalen, Belfrē Kitchen
with apples from Bower's Produce

Visit Belfrē Kitchen on just about any given day, and you'll see crates of freshly picked produce. Some have been delivered to the restaurant by local farms, while others are hand-picked by chefs at the local farmers markets. These fresh, local components form the building blocks for the eatery's seasonal menu.

During the growing season, Sous Chef Scott Whalen is known to make daily trips to the market to select fresh produce for dishes, including this delicious side that shines the spotlight on humble brussels sprouts. The dish makes full use of crisp apples from Bower's Produce, along with fresh, tender sprouts, pulling together two classic autumnal flavors in one memorable dish.

SERVES 4-6

For the coulis:

16 ounces raw peeled chestnuts*

1 tablespoon canola oil

5 medium shallots, roughly chopped

1 teaspoon plus 1 tablespoon kosher salt, divided

5 Granny Smith apples, peeled and coarsely chopped

3 tablespoons sugar

6 tablespoons apple cider vinegar, divided

2 cups water

1 teaspoon cinnamon

*Frozen raw chestnuts are available online or through specialty grocers.

To prepare the coulis:

Toast the chestnuts in a dry sauté pan until fragrant and golden. Set aside.

Heat a medium-size saucepan over medium heat and add canola oil along with the chopped shallots. Season with 1 teaspoon salt and sauté until the shallots are translucent. Add Granny Smith apples, toasted chestnuts, and sugar and stir to combine. Raise the heat to medium-high and sauté the mixture for about 5 minutes, and then reduce the heat to low and deglaze the pan with 4 tablespoons of apple cider vinegar. Continue cooking for about 15–20 minutes or until the apples are tender, stirring occasionally.

Once the apples are tender, remove the mixture from the heat and allow it to cool for 5 minutes. Add mixture to a blender jar along with water, 1 tablespoon of salt, cinnamon, and the additional 2 tablespoons of apple cider vinegar. Blend until smooth. Taste for seasoning, adding a bit more apple cider vinegar or cinnamon to taste. Chill in the fridge.

For fried shallots:

1 large shallot, thinly sliced into rings

canola oil

kosher salt

For lemon vinaigrette:

1 lemon, juiced

¼ cup champagne vinegar

½ cup canola oil

1 teaspoon kosher salt

For brussels sprouts:

8 cups brussels sprouts (about 2 pounds), cleaned and halved lengthwise

1–2 teaspoons canola oil

For the garnish:

1 Honeycrisp apple, sliced into matchsticks

1 teaspoon of fresh parsley leaves, finely chopped

2 tablespoons fresh dill leaves, stems removed

To prepare fried shallots:

Pour two inches of canola oil into a medium saucepan with high sides and heat to 350°F. Carefully drop thinly sliced shallot rings into the oil and constantly stir until they become golden brown (watch carefully, as it happens quickly).

Make sure you have a deep enough pot since the oil level will rise once you drop the shallots in.

Have a small strainer ready so you can get the shallots out of the oil. Transfer fried shallots onto a paper towel and salt immediately. Spread shallots in a single layer on a paper-towel-lined plate to stay crisp.

To prepare the lemon vinaigrette:

Combine the lemon juice, vinegar, canola oil, and salt in a small container with a lid. Shake it up or whisk it until the vinaigrette is emulsified.

To prepare the brussels sprouts:

Preheat the oven to 400°F.

Heat a large cast-iron skillet over medium heat and coat the bottom with 1–2 teaspoons of canola oil. Working in batches, carefully add brussels sprouts to the skillet cut-side down and cook for a few minutes undisturbed until they are light golden brown and partially cooked. Transfer brussels sprouts to a baking tray.

When all of your sprouts have been browned, place the baking tray into the preheated oven and roast for 6–8 minutes, or until your brussels sprouts have reached your ideal level of tenderness. Remove them from the oven, transfer them to a large mixing bowl, and immediately toss the hot brussels sprouts with lemon vinaigrette. Taste for salt, adding if needed.

To serve: Spread apple coulis on a large serving platter. Pour roasted brussels sprouts over the top. Sprinkle with the fried shallots and matchstick apples and garnish with parsley and dill.

Roasted Sweet Potato and Pears with Goat Cheese Labneh and Pickled Currants

Chef Karen Bell, Bavette La Boucherie
with produce from Produce with Purpose

For years, Chef Karen Bell has challenged diners' palates with artfully prepared dishes that pay homage to the simplicity and quality of Wisconsin ingredients. Her talents have earned her countless accolades, including honors as a James Beard Award finalist for Best Chef Midwest. This excellent autumnal dish is a fine example. Flavors blend harmoniously, with the sweetness of sweet potato, pear, and honey offsetting the slightly spicy nduja, the goat cheese labneh adding tang and richness, and the pickled currents offering a beautiful pop of acid.

SERVES 4

For the goat cheese labneh:

4 cups Greek yogurt, plain

1 tablespoon kosher salt

2 tablespoons lemon juice

1 cup goat cheese, crumbled

For the pickled currants:

1 cup water

1 cup white wine vinegar

2 tablespoons sugar

½ tablespoon kosher salt

¾ teaspoon pickling spice

1 cup currants

For the nduja honey:

½ pound nduja

1 teaspoon extra virgin olive oil

2 tablespoons honey

To prepare the labneh:

At least 12 hours prior, combine yogurt, salt, and lemon juice into a bowl until evenly mixed. Transfer the mixture into a strainer lined with cheesecloth to strain into the bowl overnight in the refrigerator. To finish the labneh, mix the firmed yogurt mixture with goat cheese and keep chilled until ready to serve.

To prepare the pickled currants:

Combine all ingredients (except the currants) into a small stock pot and bring to a boil. Remove the liquid from the heat and strain over the currants into a bowl. Place the bowl into the refrigerator overnight, straining the liquid from the currants and allowing them to air-dry prior to serving.

To prepare the nduja honey:

In a nonstick skillet over medium heat, combine nduja with oil and cook, breaking up the nduja into a fine mixture, similar to ground beef. Add honey and continue to stir and mix until evenly combined and warmed.

For the sweet potatoes and pears:

2 sweet potatoes, washed and scrubbed

1 teaspoon sumac

½ teaspoon kosher salt

a drizzle of honey

lemon juice, one squeeze

2 pears, washed

2 tablespoons neutral oil

For plating:

2 cups watercress leaves or arugula

1 tablespoon extra virgin olive oil

To prepare the sweet potatoes and pears:

Preheat the oven to 400°F.

Cut the sweet potatoes in half the long way, and then cut each half into four or six long wedges, depending on the size of the sweet potato. Put in a bowl and toss with the sumac, most of the salt, a drizzle of honey, and a squeeze of lemon juice. Toss and put on a sheet tray; roast in the oven for 25–30 minutes, until lightly browned and tender. Cut the pears in quarters the long way and remove the core. Toss with a pinch of salt and a little oil, and then place them onto another sheet tray and roast for 15 minutes or until slightly softened. Once cooled slightly, cut the pears into smaller wedges.

To plate the dish:

Spread a generous spoonful of labneh at the base of a plate. Dress a small amount of watercress or arugula with some olive oil and place on top of the labneh. Next, arrange four or five wedges of sweet potato and three or four wedges of pear on top, and garnish with approximately 1 teaspoon of pickled currants. To finish, drizzle a tablespoon or two of the warmed nduja honey around the plate.

Folk Tree Farm

Washington Island, Wisconsin
facebook.com/folktreewashingtonisland

Having been surrounded by farms and farming heritage his entire life, Casey Dahl was a natural to enter the agricultural realm. His interest in environmental issues, love for the outdoors, and natural curiosity led him to train at the Michael Fields Agricultural Institute in East Troy, Wisconsin, where he met Shawn Murray, a University of Wisconsin–Madison graduate who also had an interest in small-scale, sustainable organic farming.

The two acquired their first Oberhasli dairy goats in 2009 and began making cheese and soaps. At the same time, they continued their

FOLK TREE FARM

education, working and managing a variety of small farms including Prairie Dock, LotFotL, Turtle Creek Gardens, and Rohrganics. But when a chance connection with Russell Rolffs of Hoot Blossom Farm led to an invitation to consider starting a farm on Washington Island, they decided to make the move to the island just off the northeast corner of Door County Peninsula. There, they purchased a twenty-one-acre property (along with a homestead that dates back to the late 1800s) and established Folk Tree Farm.

Currently they farm about two and a half acres on the property with organic methods, growing a wide variety of vegetables, fruit and nut trees, and shiitake mushrooms, as well as pasturing Oberhasli dairy goats. They are also avid participants in growing trials for the University of Wisconsin Seed to Kitchen program and Seed Savers, actively reporting on yields, disease resistance, and success rates with various vegetable varieties. On the side, the couple manages an orchard of cider apples for Island Orchard Cider, planting and pruning trees in early spring, tending the orchard, and harvesting the apples for the Ellison Bay cidery in autumn.

As farmers on a small island, Casey and Shawn take their roles providing fresh, organically produced vegetables for their community seriously, paying close attention to their environmental impact and working to keep agriculture and agricultural history alive on the island. Currently about 40 percent of their produce is sold to Hotel Washington, with the remainder sold at the local Gathering Ground Farmers Market.

Dahl says he's regularly impressed by how committed the chefs at Hotel Washington are to using as much produce as possible from Washington Island. That's evidenced in the manner in which they work with the farms and design their menus. In the fall, the farmers from both Folk Tree and Hoot Blossom Farms meet with the chefs to discuss the previous season and begin planning for the next. Over the years, as the chefs and farmers have worked together, they've been able to collaborate to create menus that are designed around the types of produce that grow well in the area. That includes staples like strawberries, shelling and sugar snap peas, green beans, brassicas (kale and broccolini), root vegetables (carrots, beets), and fresh shelling beans, zucchini, and cucumbers.

The kitchen staff work with the farm to ensure that large harvests don't go to waste. If there is an overabundance of yellow squash during the peak of the season, the chefs work quickly to add specials like stuffed squash and squash soup to the menu.

Shawn says that life on a farm, particularly in such a tight-knit community, is uniquely rewarding. Not only can their family enjoy the satisfaction of looking out over fields of produce, orchards filled with fruit, and the goats as they frolic on pasture, but they also have the opportunity to interact with both local residents and tourists who come to shop their wares at the farmers market.

Between April and October, curious visitors to Washington Island have the unique opportunity to rent out the upstairs of the farmhouse through Airbnb. The peaceful homestead offers folks an opportunity to take a break from the bustle of city life and learn more about farming and life on Washington Island.

Seared Broccolini with Sourdough Pearls, Pickled Green Garlic, Aleppo, and Mimolette

Ian Milosek, Ana Randall, and Weston Nutkins, Hotel Washington with vegetables from Hoot Blossom and Folk Tree Farms

On Washington Island, summers are cool and winters are harsh. Crops start late in the season and take time to mature. While others are harvesting the first of their summer crop, the island is still savoring spring vegetables. At times, the slow pace is a hassle; however, it can also be a blessing, as the extended springtime weather allows for enjoying a larger variety of plates with ingredients like foraged spring ramps and green garlic.

This broccolini dish is a celebration of the first harvest of broccolini from Folk Tree Farm, usually in late June. It's an elevated take on the broccoli and cheese that Mom used to make, allowing the fresh flavor of the broccolini to shine through. Sourdough pearls stand in for breadcrumbs, and the French Mimolette cheese leaves Mom's cheddar in the dust. Meanwhile, the dish is enhanced by a chef-inspired burst of spice from earthy Aleppo pepper and a balancing acidic pop from pickled green garlic sourced from Hoot Blossom Farm. It's an ingredient that hearkens back to spring and gives the dish a little something extra.

Together this dish is one, but every layer shines through with its own voice.

SERVES 4

For the pickled green garlic:

3 green garlic stalks

½ cup champagne vinegar

½ cup sugar

½ cup cold water

For the sourdough pearls:

4 cups of canola oil

½ cup of sourdough starter

⅛ cup water

kosher salt

To prepare pickled green garlic:

Trim green garlic so that only the round stalks are left. Place them in a small heat-proof vessel. Mix vinegar, sugar, and ½ cup water in a pot and bring just to a boil. Remove the brine from the heat and pour it over green garlic. Allow the garlic to remain in the brine for 4 hours or overnight.

To prepare the sourdough pearls:

In a large pot, bring 4 cups of canola oil to 350°F.

Prepare a plate lined with paper towels. Mix the sourdough starter with ½ cup of water and stir until smooth.

When the oil is hot, hold a sieve over the pot of oil and carefully pour the starter into the sieve so that the sourdough drops through into the oil. As the sourdough pearls begin to float, transfer them to the paper-towel-lined plate. Immediately sprinkle them with salt.

For the broccolini:

1 tablespoon neutral oil (grapeseed or canola)

1 bundle broccolini, leaves removed and bottoms trimmed

kosher salt and pepper, to taste

For plating:

½ pound French Mimolette cheese, finely shredded

1 teaspoon Aleppo pepper

salt (this is the perfect time to pull out your fancy finishing salt)

To prepare the broccolini:

Start by heating a large cast-iron skillet on the stove over medium-high heat. When the cast iron is hot, add a tablespoon of oil to the pan. Place the broccolini into the pan, season it with salt and pepper, and sear until browned on each side.

To assemble:

Transfer the broccolini to a plate and garnish with the shredded Mimolette, sourdough pearls, Aleppo pepper, and finely shaved pickled green garlic. Top it off with a pinch of finishing salt.

HOOT BLOSSOM FARM

Hoot Blossom Farm

Washington Island, Wisconsin
facebook.com/hootblossom

In 2016, Alessandra and Russell Rolffs traveled to Washington Island for the summer. The former teachers had been living in Milwaukee while Alessandra worked on her doctoral degree in creative writing at the University of Wisconsin–Milwaukee. While they were there, they met Jeannie Kokes, owner of Hotel Washington Restaurant and Studio. Jeannie had just purchased a tract of land and was looking for someone to cultivate it and grow vegetables for the restaurant. The couple took her up on her offer, agreeing to spend the summer on the island and help her start the farm.

They took what had been a meadow, tilled the soil, and began growing a cadre of vegetables. As the summer waned, they realized they'd fallen in love with life on the island, so they decided to stay, transitioning to full-time farmers over the course of the next two years.

From the beginning, the main goal for Hoot Blossom Farm was to supply vegetables for the hotel, which is located on a thirty-five-square-mile island located just off the northeast tip of Door Peninsula in northern Wisconsin. Currently, just over 30 percent of the crops grown on the farm support the restaurant, with the remainder sold at the Island Farmers Market and local grocery store. In the spring, the Rolffs maintain a native plant nursery, which they use to raise seedlings to sell to locals for their gardens. They also grow fields of cut flowers, which they sell to

locals through a subscription bouquet service that operates on a similar model as a community-supported agriculture (CSA) program.

During the farm's first season, Hoot Blossom was the only local farm supplying the restaurant, so the Rolffs would sit down with the chefs at the beginning of the season and plan the farm's crops based on what the restaurant needed to make it through the tourism season (May through October).

In addition to meeting the hotel's needs, the Rolffs concentrated on making the most of the short growing season on the

HOOT BLOSSOM FARM

island. They planted asparagus to harvest in the spring, as well as short-season brassicas. They also grew ten different varieties of broccoli (including broccoli rabe, broccolini, and bok choy) and a dozen types of radishes to offer the chefs a range of options. The Rolffs, who operate the farm using organic practices, note that the cyclical nature of farming, along with the privilege of feeding and nurturing the soil, watching vegetables grow up from seed, and carving out an intimate relationship with the land is among the many rewards of their second career.

In 2018, the hotel began sourcing from a second farm, Folk Tree Farm. To bring efficiency to the process, the Rolffs began meeting with Folk Tree Farm operators Shawn Murray and Casey Dahl to plan the crops for each respective farm. The Rolffs had devised an efficient system for growing lettuces, so they assumed responsibility for the greens, along with varieties of peppers and cherry tomatoes. Meanwhile, Folk Tree took on the broccoli, cauliflower, and kale.

The farmers contribute to the food preservation efforts at the restaurant by taking on activities like smoking and drying Beaver Dam and Jimmy Nardello peppers for use in restaurant dishes. Even as Hoot Blossom Farm has asserted its independence from Hotel Washington over the years, the Rolffs note that collaboration and maintaining a unified vision for both the farm and the restaurant remains a top priority as they plan for the future.

The Rolffs have made their own imprint on the local agricultural community, co-founding Gathering Ground, a nonprofit dedicated to promoting sustainable agriculture on Washington Island. The organization has operated a farmers market on the island since 2017.

John Adams Old Place

Ask the locals about the acre of land on which Hoot Blossom Farm resides, and they're likely to refer to it as "John Adams's old place." The cabin on the property dates back to the early twentieth century when it was part of the Green Gate Farm. The farm was tended by an African American gentleman named John Quincy Adams. He worked as a chauffeur for Mr. Gentry, a Chicagoan who moved to Washington Island when his doctor prescribed country living as a cure for his ailments. He came to the island and planted an orchard of cherry trees, which Adams would tend during the summer months.

In the 1960s, Gentry sold the farm to the Ulms family. When they decided to eliminate the orchard, they asked Adams to cut down all of the trees. Adams's wife, Gert, is quoted in a local publication as saying that the chore was like "cutting down his children."

After he chopped down the trees he'd tended for decades, he was asked to leave the farm. But a group of local islanders gathered together in his defense, purchasing a farmstead just down the street for him and his wife. A few of the apple trees he planted on the farmstead are still thriving. The locals call them Adams Apples.

Entrées

Recipes

Featured Farms

WISCONSIN GRASS-FED BEEF COOPERATIVE

River Valley Ranch

Burlington, Wisconsin
rvrvalley.com

For years, restaurateur William Rose had struggled with sourcing high-quality mushrooms for his restaurant in Illinois. So, in 1976, he decided to take things into his own hands, establishing a mushroom farm in a small barn near the Fox River. His goal? To provide the highest-quality mushrooms possible to markets and area restaurants. With help from his son, Eric Rose, who swiftly assumed operations for the farm, business grew, eventually prompting the move to a larger production facility as well as the addition of a farm store on location.

In the late 2000s, after their portobello salsa was featured on Food Network's *Food Finds* show, business took off. What had begun as a two-man operation for white button mushrooms expanded to include three certified organic mushroom varieties, along with shiitake and oyster, lion's mane, and maitake mushrooms, all of which are grown without the use of chemicals to deter pests and other invasive microorganisms. River Valley also plants up to twenty-five acres of pesticide- and chemical-free vegetables and operates an on-site commercial kitchen where they produce pickled mushrooms and other vegetable-based products. They operate a farm store in Burlington, Wisconsin, and a farmer-owned grocery store and home delivery service in Chicago, Illinois.

River Valley Ranch organic mushrooms include portobello, cremini, and white button, which are grown year-round in its five growing houses, where temperature, humidity, and airflow are carefully controlled. The farm handles its own compost production, which is produced on-site using sustainable methods.

Over the years, Eric hired dozens of employees to work with him on the farm. Among them was Jennifer Brown, whom he initially hired in 1997 to work part-time at the farm store. She enjoyed the work, and by the following season, she had taken on responsibilities working in the mushroom

gardens. The more she learned, the more her interest in farming grew, so she enrolled in the horticulture program at Gateway Technical College in Kenosha, Wisconsin. From there, she began working at the farmers markets, where she fell in love with the fast-paced environment and inter-acting with customers. Currently, Jennifer oversees operations at River Valley, which produces as many as fifteen thousand pounds of mush-rooms per week during the spring, summer, and fall growing seasons (May through October).

Today, River Valley Ranch holds the honor of being the longest-operating commercial mushroom farm in the Midwest, supplying fresh mushrooms to countless restaurants in Milwaukee, Lake Geneva, and Chicago.

Vegetable Tower

Executive Chef Joshua North, The Abbey Resort
with mushrooms from River Valley Ranch

This dish embodies locally sourced vegan simplicity. Earthy portobello mushrooms from River Valley Ranch come together with farm-fresh sweet peppers, summer squash, and a rich parsnip puree in this visually appealing display of summer bounty.

Appropriate as a main dish, a side, or a starter for a dinner party, this fun vegetable-centric dish can be modified to make the best use of whatever is fresh at the farmers market. When making substitutions, just be sure to maintain a variety of flavors and textures.

SERVES 4

For the glaze:

8 ounces eight-year aged balsamic vinegar

For the puree:

6 parsnips, peeled and diced (reserve peelings in ice water)

extra virgin olive oil, plus 2 tablespoons, divided

1 teaspoon kosher salt

additional kosher salt and black pepper, to taste

For the vegetables:

4 large portobello mushrooms (4–5 inches wide), stems removed and discarded

1 large red bell pepper, sliced into 3–4 large pieces

1 large green bell pepper, sliced into 3–4 large pieces

To prepare balsamic vinegar glaze:

Place the vinegar in a small saucepan over medium heat. Bring to a gentle boil, and then reduce heat to medium-low and allow it to simmer until reduced by three-quarters, at least 20 minutes. It will be thick enough to coat the back of a spoon. Remove from heat and allow to cool. Set aside.

To prepare parsnip puree:

Preheat oven to 450° (convection, if available).

Remove parsnip peelings from the ice water and pat them dry. Place enough olive oil in a small sauté pan to cover the bottom of the pan and place it over medium heat. Place the parsnip peels in the pan and cook until crisp.

Meanwhile, place the diced parsnips in a saucepan, cover them with water, and season with about 1 teaspoon of salt. Bring to a simmer and cook until parsnips are tender. When they are cooked, drain the water from the pan and add 2 tablespoons of olive oil, salt, and pepper, mashing with a fork until no lumps remain.

To prepare the vegetables:

Place remaining vegetables on a sheet pan in a single layer, drizzling them lightly with olive oil and seasoning them with salt and pepper on both sides. Place them in the oven and bake for 7 minutes.

1 medium red onion, peeled and root end removed, sliced into ¼-inch thick slices

1 medium zucchini squash, bias cut into ⅜ inch thick slices

1 medium yellow squash, bias cut into ⅜ inch thick slices

1 bunch of asparagus spears, ends trimmed

extra virgin olive oil

kosher salt and black pepper, to taste

To assemble the vegetable tower:

Place mushrooms at the base of each plate, gill-side up. Divide all parsnip puree into equal amounts, placing it inside the mushrooms' gills. Arrange the remaining vegetables on top of the puree in the order of your choosing. Arrange the asparagus alongside. Drizzle with balsamic reduction and top with crisp parsnip peelings.

Confit Potatoes and Leeks with Grilled Mushrooms and Horseradish Vinaigrette

The chef team at Wickman House
with fresh vegetables from the Wickman House Garden

This composed vegetarian dish is a luscious treat featuring pieces of tender leek-scented potatoes and hearty grilled mushrooms balanced by the slight zip and acidity of horseradish vinaigrette. At Wickman House, it's made with farm-fresh vegetables picked from the restaurant's garden.

Even on their own, the confit potatoes and leeks are a versatile dish to add to your repertoire. They are positively indulgent served as a side dish topped with freshly cracked black pepper, crème fraîche, fresh thyme leaves, and a grating of lemon zest. Alternatively, if you happen to have leftovers, you can smash the potato leek mixture together and fry it until golden on both sides. Serve the crisp, leeky potatoes topped with a poached farm-fresh egg and roasted asparagus or another seasonal vegetable.

SERVES 4

For the horseradish vinaigrette:

8 ounces prepared horseradish

1 tablespoon Dijon mustard

½ cup apple cider vinegar

squeeze of lemon and a touch of zest

pinch of kosher salt and pepper

1 garlic clove (optional)

½ teaspoon caraway seeds, toasted (optional)

1 cup grapeseed oil

½ cup extra virgin olive oil

honey (optional)

To prepare the horseradish vinaigrette:

Place all the ingredients except the oil and honey (if using) in a blender and blend on high until smooth. Then add the grapeseed oil in a slow, steady stream. Once it is incorporated, add the olive oil in the same manner until all of it is in the blender. Turn the blender off and taste. Add more salt to taste and a touch of honey if you need to calm the brightness down. You can also add extra Dijon mustard for more punch. The vinaigrette can be made ahead of time and stored in a glass jar in the refrigerator, where it will keep for up to two weeks. You'll have more of this flavorful vinaigrette than you need for the recipe; try it on sliced cucumbers, roasted root vegetables, or sturdy greens like escarole or radicchio.

To prepare the confit cure:

Finely grind all spices and mix with the salt.

To prepare the confit:

Preheat the oven to 350°F.

For the confit cure:

1 cup kosher salt

2 teaspoons black peppercorns

5 allspice berries

2 cloves

¼ teaspoon dried ginger, ground

For the confit potatoes and leeks:

4–5 large Yukon gold potatoes

1 tablespoon and a large pinch of confit cure

1 large leek

2 quarts of extra virgin olive oil, and maybe a bit more

For the grilled mushrooms:

1 pound hearty mushrooms such as portobello or lion's mane, trimmed

1 teaspoon high-quality olive oil

kosher salt and pepper, to taste

fresh lemon juice (optional)

Scrub and wash the potatoes. Cut them into large wedges and toss in a bowl with 1 tablespoon and a large three-finger pinch of the confit cure. Stir or toss to completely coat all surfaces of the potatoes. Let the potatoes rest in a colander for 30 minutes to 1 hour to drain.

While the potatoes are draining, peel off the outer layer of the leek. Trim the root end and the tips of the green end and discard, keeping the bulk of the green tops. Cut the leek in half lengthwise. Rest leeks cut side down on a cutting board and, with a sharp knife, cut them into ½–1-inch ribbons. Submerge the chopped leeks in cool water and agitate well. Drain the leeks into a strainer and return them to the bowl. Fill the bowl with cool water and agitate again. Repeat if necessary to completely clean the leeks of any residual dirt. Drain on a towel and pat dry.

On a stovetop, place the potatoes, leeks, and 2 quarts of olive oil into a large, heavy oven-safe pot with a lid (a Dutch oven works well). Heat slowly over moderately low heat uncovered until the potatoes begin to show a slight hint of a sizzle. Turn the heat off, put a lid on the pot, and place it in the oven on a low rack. Set a timer for 20 minutes. After 20 minutes, turn the oven down to 250°F and set another 20-minute timer. At the end of the second 20 minutes, lift the lid (take care to lift it away from your face to avoid burning yourself with the accumulated steam) and check to see how tender the potatoes are by pinching them with a pair of tongs. Be careful not to burn yourself with hot oil. The potatoes and leeks should be getting soft now. If they are not, turn down the heat to 225°F and check for soft potatoes in 10-minute increments.

Once the potatoes are soft, remove the confit from the oven and allow the potatoes and leeks to cool with the lid off. If serving soon, let them sit in the oil as long as possible. Remove the potatoes and leeks from the very warm fat, allowing the excess fat to drip off back into the pot.

To prepare the mushrooms:

While the confit cools, lightly brush mushrooms with the olive oil and season moderately with salt and pepper. Grill the mushrooms on medium-high until the mushrooms are softened with a nice char. Test for seasoning and adjust accordingly. If it's a bit too salty for your taste, sprinkle with some fresh lemon juice.

To plate:

Drizzle a bit of vinaigrette on the plate. Top with pieces of potatoes and leeks and a nice portion of grilled mushrooms. Drizzle a bit more of the vinaigrette on top.

Yet another option:

Take the entire dish to another level by sautéing chopped tatsoi or bok choy with olive oil and a bit of salt. Pile the hearty greens on top of the dish, along with a drizzle of horseradish vinaigrette or a bit of fried giardiniera.

Rare Earth Farm

Belgium, Wisconsin
rareearthfarm.com

Steve Young thought he'd be in a position to start slowing down by now. But his passion for farming has kept him in the fray, even as challenges (like staffing issues) related to the COVID-19 pandemic have impacted his business. Every winter, he still looks forward to the hours spent perusing seed catalogs and considering his options for the upcoming growing season. He calls it a "passion gone totally out of control."

Steve says his interest in plants and the science behind growing vegetables hearkens back to his childhood, growing up alongside parents who were avid gardeners. His appreciation for fresh vegetables and gardening followed him throughout college and into his adult life. But

RARE EARTH FARM

he didn't pursue farming as a profession until 1990. At that point, he'd been working for years as a technology educator and engineer in the corporate world and was looking for a change. So he began pursuing his agricultural interests on the side. He started with a small garden in which he grew enough produce to support a small community-supported agriculture program and some sales at local farmers markets. His business doubled by year two, prompting him to purchase twenty acres of land in Ozaukee County, where Rare Earth now resides.

As business grew, Steve gradually moved away from selling at the farmers market and focused more exclusively on his CSA program, which quickly became the bread and butter of the farm. By 1997, he was able to leave his job and transition to farming full time.

He began the farm with a diverse collection of crops, both heirloom and hybrid, in an effort to offer his CSA customers a robust selection of vegetables throughout the season. But, like every farmer, he also paid attention to crops like chicory and radicchio, which he found grew particularly well in the microclimate on his land, situated just a few miles from Lake Michigan. To accommodate sensitive crops like fava beans and basil, which don't do as well in the wildly fluctuating weather conditions, he dedicated a quarter acre of land to in-ground greenhouses, which he uses to extend the season for crops like greens well into the winter months.

Although Rare Earth has never been certified as an organic farm, Steve has always relied on growing methods that preserve the health of the soil and contribute to the overall health of the farm's environment. That includes eschewing chemical inputs for crop protection and soil fertility and using materials that comply with the USDA's National Organic Program (NOP). Soil testing, composting, and the use of cover crops are all commonplace, as is integrated pest management employed to protect crops from insects. Meanwhile, he promotes pollination—and produces a supply of raw honey—by maintaining beehives on the property as well.

Despite the farm's reliance on its CSA program, Rare Earth has also maintained long-term relationships with select restaurants. In the mid-1990s, Steve focused on larger accounts, including The American Club

in Kohler. But he also branched out to include family-owned eateries like Pandl's in Bayside and the Bartolotta Restaurants, where he met chefs like Zachary Baker, now co-owner of Ca'Lucchenzo, who has remained a loyal customer for most of a decade.

Steve says that he has always enjoyed working with restaurants, particularly since chefs naturally have an interest in and appreciation for the wide variety of vegetables that Rare Earth produces. He's had the privilege of enjoying the occasional meal at restaurants like Ca'Lucchenzo, where his vegetables are transformed into edible works of art.

As Steve looks to the future of his farm and considers ways to balance his workload, he would like to focus more on growing vegetables for local restaurants, delve more deeply into beekeeping, and transition to a farming lifestyle that still provides a daily connection to the land but allows him to rely less on staff to keep the farm operational.

Fava Bean Risotto

Chef Zachary Baker, Ca'Lucchenzo
with fava beans from Rare Earth Farm

If you've never experienced the wonder of fresh fava beans, this recipe is a must-try. Chef Zachary Baker has deftly incorporated the delicate summer delicacy into a risotto that allows their flavor to shine. The bean's light herbaceous flavor and velvety texture meld perfectly with the rich creaminess of the risotto. Try pairing this dish with Bianco di Custoza, a white wine from the Veneto region of northeastern Italy.

SERVES 4 AS A MAIN COURSE OR 6 AS A FIRST COURSE

For the risotto:

4 pounds fava beans, fresh in their pods

12 cups blonde chicken stock (see note)

½ cup yellow onion, finely minced

4 tablespoons extra virgin olive oil

3 tablespoons unsalted butter, divided

1½ cup carnaroli rice, preferably Acquerello

1 cup dry white wine

1½ teaspoons kosher salt

½ cup Parmigiano-Reggiano, finely grated

10 fresh mint leaves

juice from half a lemon

To prepare the fava beans:

Bring 4 quarts of water, salted to taste like the ocean, to a rolling boil, and prepare an ice bath for cooling the blanched beans.

Shuck the fava beans from their pods. The beans will have a pale green-yellow skin on them; leave this covering intact for now. Blanch half of the beans at a time, allowing them to cook in the boiling water for 2 minutes and immediately transferring them to the ice bath to cool. Peel the skins from the fava beans to reveal the bright green bean inside. Usually a little pinch with your fingertips will be enough to get them to pop out of their skins. You should have about 2 cups of fava beans when you are finished.

SARA STATHAS

To prepare the risotto:

Bring the chicken stock to a simmer and keep it hot on a burner close to you. In a 6-quart Dutch oven, slowly sweat the minced onion in 4 tablespoons of olive oil and 2 tablespoons of butter. Take your time to cook the onion through until translucent and soft, but not browned. Add the rice at this point, and continue to cook the onion and rice over low heat for about 2 minutes until the rice has been thoroughly coated in the butter and oil and has become shiny.

Raise the heat to medium-high and add the white wine and the salt; cook while stirring constantly until the wine has mostly evaporated (about 2 minutes). Begin adding the warm stock, with the first addition being enough to cover the rice by about an inch, and continue to cook at a brisk simmer while stirring constantly. Once the stock has been mostly absorbed, add more hot stock, about 1 cup at a time. Each time, wait to add more stock until the previous addition has been mostly absorbed.

Continue to do this for about 20–25 minutes, until the rice is cooked through but still retains a slight al dente chew in the center. The texture at this point should be more on the soupy side than the sticky and stiff side. You may not need to use all the stock.

Add the cooked fava beans, the Parmigiano, the mint leaves (tear them as you are adding them to the risotto), 1 tablespoon of butter, and the juice of half a lemon to the risotto. Stir vigorously at this point to allow the cheese and butter to blend with the warm broth around the rice. Add a couple tablespoons of hot stock to adjust the consistency if the risotto has gotten too stiff. The finished risotto in the pot should always be flat; if it is thick enough to pile up or hold a spoon up, add more stock. Serve immediately on warmed plates.

Note: If using store-bought chicken stock, use 8 cups of stock to 4 cups of water. This ratio prevents the finished risotto from becoming too rich and "meaty," overwhelming the fava beans. Also do this if your homemade chicken stock is very rich or dark from roasting the chicken bones or from an overliberal use of carrots. If vegetable stock is necessary, make a simple stock using only onions, celery, and leeks. Do not use carrots or tomatoes, which will impart both unwanted color and flavor to the risotto.

Red Door Family Farm

Athens, Wisconsin
reddoorfamilyfarm.com

Stacey and Tenzin Botsford didn't exactly have farming on their list of life goals. For twelve years, they traveled the world, guiding week-long white-water rafting adventures for well-to-do tourists in destinations like Costa Rica, Mexico, Canada, and New Zealand. The work appealed to their love of the outdoors, but it left them wanting something more. Throughout their travels, they'd encountered numerous industrious people who worked hard at jobs that not only allowed them to make a living and care for their families but also benefited their communities. These were happy people who took pride in what they did and whose daily grind served a higher purpose.

So the Botsfords moved back to the United States in search of work that would offer them a similar sense of fulfillment. They worked their way through Idaho, where Tenzin found work as a river surveyor and Stacey worked part-time at restaurants and a farm. Eventually they found themselves in Oregon, where they apprenticed and managed an organic pro-

duce farm and, ultimately, a diversified organic meat and dairy farm. The work inspired them and pushed them to start a farm of their own with the goals of caring for the land, growing food for their community, and making a living for themselves.

In 2013, they moved to the Wausau area, where they secured forty acres on a land contract. They built a home on the acreage and began growing a variety of vegetables using low-till farming methods, cover crops, crop rotation, and natural pest management. By 2015, they launched their first CSA program and began selling their produce at local farmers markets. Red Door Family Farm was born.

Today the Botsfords farm about twelve acres of the land, with a focus on strawberries, carrots, heirloom tomatoes, broccoli, cauliflower, and winter squash. They also raise a small number of chickens for meat and eggs. They've continued sales at the market and their CSA program, as well as supplying produce for local restaurants, including Van Acres and Red Eye Brewing Company.

They've taken pride in seeing their ultra-fresh produce transformed into creative dishes that show the chefs' appreciation for what they do. Over time, they've developed a deep admiration for chefs who understand farming, appreciate seasonality, and assist them by purchasing surplus vegetables to use for specials during the height of the growing season. They also work with the Wisconsin Food Hub Cooperative (WFHC) in Waupaca, which distributes local produce to restaurants, retail establishments, and other organizations.

Red Door has collaborated with other farms, including Cattail Organics and Stoney Acres Farm, sharing produce to round out CSA boxes, collaborating on local projects, and working together with the common goal of strengthening the local agricultural system.

Stacey says that although the day-to-day work on the farm can be tedious, when they stand back and look at the big picture, they feel gratitude and fulfillment in being able to contribute to their local community and nourish people with fresh local food.

Cauliflower Curry with Beluga Lentils and Carrot Puree

Chef Nathan Bychinski, Red Eye Brewing Company
with vegetables from Red Door Family Farm

This flavorful vegetarian curry brings together hearty lentils, cauliflower, and carrots in a dish that's rife with warming spices and hearty flavor. You'll be happy to have extra curried golden raisins on hand. They offer a delicious pop of saffron for spiced rice, but they're also great for livening up an ordinary batch of chicken salad.

SERVES 4

For the curried golden raisins:

1 cup golden raisins

1 piece ginger

5 garlic cloves

1 bay leaf

1 jalapeño

2 cinnamon sticks

2 star anise

2 Granny Smith apples, halved

2 sprigs of thyme

⅛ cup of rice wine vinegar

¼ cup of sugar

2 tablespoons curry powder

kosher salt, to taste

lemon juice, to taste

For the beluga lentils:

½ cup beluga lentils

1 onion, half roughly chopped, half small diced

2 stalks of celery, 1 roughly chopped, 1 small diced

2 carrots, 1 roughly chopped, 1 small diced

2 sprigs thyme

1 cinnamon stick

To prepare the raisins:

Set raisins in a container that can handle high heat, reserving for later. Combine all other ingredients in a saucepan, cover with water, and bring to a boil. Turn down to a simmer and continue cooking for 30 minutes. While the liquid is still hot, strain it and pour it over the raisins. Set aside. Drain before using as garnish.

To prepare the lentils:

Place lentils in a sauce pot with the roughly cut onion, celery, and carrot. Add a sachet d'epices, containing the thyme, cinnamon stick, peppercorns, bay leaf, and star anise. Fill the pot with warm water, covering the contents by about 2 inches. Place on the stove over medium-high heat. When it begins to boil, turn heat down to a light simmer. Cook lentils for about 20 minutes, until al dente. While lentils are cooking, cut remaining onion, celery, and carrot into a small dice, keeping separate. Sauté each vegetable starting with onion, followed by celery, and finally carrot, creating a mirepoix. Cool lentils and mirepoix, and then mix. Reserve for later. When you reheat the lentils, start by melting a tablespoon of butter in the pan, and then add lentils and season to taste with salt, pepper, lemon juice, and persillade.

10 peppercorns

1 bay leaf

1 star anise

1 tablespoon butter, more as needed

kosher salt, to taste

black pepper, to taste

lemon juice, to taste

persillade (see recipe on page 130)

For the cauliflower:

1 head cauliflower

olive oil

kosher salt, to taste

freshly ground pepper, to taste

lemon juice, to taste

For the carrot purée:

6 medium carrots, cut into 1-inch rounds

2 cinnamon sticks

1 piece ginger

3 garlic cloves

1 bay leaf

2 star anise

1 jalapeño

10 peppercorns

2 sprigs of thyme

2-3 tablespoons granulated sugar

¼ cup rice wine vinegar

3 tablespoons madras curry powder

3-4 tablespoons butter

kosher salt, to taste

lemon juice, to taste

For the garnish:

sliced almonds

micro cilantro or fresh cilantro leaves

SHELBY CHAMPAGNE PHOTOGRAPHY

To prepare the cauliflower:

Preheat the oven to 400°F.

Cut cauliflower into slabs so that at least one side has a flat edge. Coat with olive oil and season with salt, pepper, and lemon juice. Place in the oven and cook for 10–15 minutes or until fork tender. Let cool down and reserve for later.

To prepare the carrot puree:

Place carrots in a saucepan, cover with water. Make a sachet d'epices with cinnamon, ginger, garlic, bay leaf, star anise, jalapeño, peppercorns, and thyme. Place in the pot with carrots. Add sugar, vinegar, and madras curry to the pot. Bring to a boil and cook carrots until tender. Using a blender, puree carrots with 3–4 tablespoons of butter, using some of the remaining liquid from the pan as needed. Season with salt and lemon juice. Reserve in a small saucepan for later, keeping warm.

Putting it all together:

Reheat cauliflower in the oven. In a bowl, start with a scoop of the hot carrot puree, followed by lentils. Place cauliflower on lentils and garnish with curried golden raisins, almonds, and micro cilantro if available.

Persillade

This pesto-like sauce is a foundation in French kitchens. Composed of parsley, garlic, and oil (and sometimes lemons, capers, or even anchovies), it's a vital element in a sauté cook's mise en place. Use it for finishing soups, rubbing on the outside of grilled or roasted meats or fish, or simply adding a pop of flavor to vegetables.

1 bunch flat leaf parsley, stems removed
3 garlic cloves
3–4 tablespoons extra virgin olive oil
zest of one lemon

Finely chop the parsley, moving it to one side of your cutting board to reserve. Finely chop garlic and mix it together with parsley, chopping both together until they are well incorporated. Transfer the parsley/garlic mixture to a bowl and incorporate olive oil and lemon zest. Persillade will keep up to a week in an airtight container in your refrigerator.

Baby Mama Botanicals

Milwaukee, Wisconsin
babymamabotanicals.com

Melisa Hanson grew up on a hundred-acre property in Hartford, Wisconsin, near Holy Hill, where her childhood was imbued with elements of the natural world. Her mother, an avid gardener with an encyclopedic knowledge of plants, passed along her love for botanicals, a talent for foraging, and an appreciation for making food from scratch with ingredients on hand. Her father, an artisan and naturalist of sorts, passed along a respect for the land and for hard work, as well as life skills that bred ingenuity and self-sufficiency. She also benefited from the passion of neighbors who introduced her to the exquisite flavor of freshly pulled garden carrots and the sensory process behind transforming maple sap into syrup each spring.

All this, combined with her innate pragmatism and interest in self-reliance, led her to farming and growing her own food. Fueled by the desire to take control of her time and pass those values along to her children, the former high school English and science teacher began growing food and selling it at farmers markets in Colorado after her son was born in 2004. Just over two years later, she found herself at the helm of a program at an alternative high school in Milwaukee, where she managed

a garden and composting program and taught students about food security, nutrition, and botany.

To make ends meet, Melisa also spent nearly a decade working as a host and server for Odd Duck, a Milwaukee restaurant that made a name for itself serving a menu of seasonal globally inspired small plates made with locally sourced produce and proteins. It's where she connected with chefs Paul Zerkel and Lisa Kirkpatrick, who would go on to open Goodkind. Odd Duck is also where she met Daniel Jacobs and Dan Van Rite—the duo behind DanDan and EsterEv, chefs who taught her about wild foods like edible milkweed buds—and where she began sharing her wealth of lilacs and elderflowers with bar staff, allowing them to make creative syrups, tonics, and infusions.

It was while she was working part time in the evenings at Odd Duck that she founded her current urban farm, Baby Mama Botanicals, a business specializing in unique varieties of vegetables, herbs, and edible flowers, which she ramped up to full-time production during the COVID-19 pandemic in 2020.

Launching her business with such well-honed knowledge of the restaurant scene gave her unique insights into the types of products chefs wanted and how they wanted it picked, packed, and delivered. She was quickly able to create a business model that met their needs and fulfilled their wishes for more unusual items.

She also had the privilege of growing her business alongside her partner, Mark Trinitapoli, whose parallel vision for self-sufficiency and a new life for his daughter inspired him to leave his teaching career in favor of the independence and harmony that farming offered. His hard work and expertise have enhanced Melisa's ability to run a successful business; in addition, his partnership has offered her the joy of embracing the future as she enters a new phase of both life and parenthood.

Making use of an intensely planted half-acre city plot, she and Mark cultivate a wide variety of heirloom and rare varieties of vegetables, including Chinese red noodle beans, Queen of Malinalco tomatillos, rare chilies, and specialty salad greens like Claytonia and mâche, plus cut-and-come-again crops like high-end specialty herbs (anise hyssop, purple shiso, orange spice thyme, hoja santa, pepicha) and edible flowers. She also offers seasonal crops, including rhubarb, pumpkins, melons, and winter squash grown on land at her family's homestead.

To fund the required investment each growing season, Baby Mama offers seedlings for sale to the public in the late spring, as well as produce, herbs, and handmade products year-round through Milwaukee Farmers United, a local delivery service that delivers to residents in the Milwaukee metro area. But the heart and soul of her business is sales to the chefs, caterers, and food trucks who place regular orders for produce and herbs.

Melisa says she couldn't have more respect and admiration for the chefs and restaurants who've supported her, even during the pandemic, by continuing to order produce and herbs even after they'd pared down their menus to accommodate carry-out.

She also couldn't be happier with the self-sufficiency she's found through urban farming. Each day there are new surprises and discoveries in the garden and new sources for inspiration. The work is hard and the hours are long, but the pleasure of growing beautiful things, delivering smiles, and watching creative, innovative chefs turn her goods into edible works of art has become the magic that fuels an increasingly soul-filling journey.

Caprese Risotto

Chefs Paul Zerkel and Lisa Kirkpatrick, Goodkind with produce from Baby Mama Botanicals

The team at Goodkind considers Melisa Hanson of Baby Mama Botanicals an inspiration. She is a farmer, mother, and maker. She is courageous, fierce, and lovely. She also produces crops of unique produce, herbs, and greens that challenge the creativity of chefs at every restaurant she supplies. Goodkind uses a variety of her products, from edible flowers and medicinal herbs to vegetables, including her heirloom tomatoes. This risotto is an homage to her work.

You might be surprised to see tomato leaves used in this dish. Yes, they are edible. Here, they add both an herbal component and a hauntingly tomato-like element to the creamy risotto. A topping of fresh, bright caprese salad components finishes off the dish and makes it the perfect summer main dish or side with grilled vegetables, chicken, or fish.

SERVES 4-6

For the marinated tomatoes:

1 cup cherry tomatoes, halved

3 cups assorted heirloom tomatoes, wedged

1 cup extra virgin olive oil

1 teaspoon chili flakes

1 tablespoon sherry vinegar

kosher salt and pepper

For the risotto:

1 cup yellow onion, diced

2 ounces neutral oil

1 bay leaf

1 tablespoon garlic, minced

2 cups Carnaroli rice

1 cup dry white wine

4–6 cups chicken stock, warmed

kosher salt and pepper

4 ounces butter

2 cups fresh tomato leaves (juiced or blanched and pureed)

For the garnish:

8–16 ounces burrata

1 cup basil leaves

sea salt

To prepare the marinated tomatoes:

Mix the tomatoes, olive oil, chili flakes, and sherry vinegar together in a medium-size bowl. Season to taste with salt and pepper and allow to marinate at room temperature while you prepare the risotto.

To prepare the risotto:

In a 6–8-quart saucepan or Dutch oven, sauté the onions in oil on low heat until translucent. Add the bay leaf, garlic, and rice and sauté for 3 more minutes, stirring to coat the rice with oil. Raise the heat to medium-high and add the wine, stirring until it has mostly evaporated. Add enough warm stock to cover the rice and season with salt and pepper. Cook the rice in stock at a brisk simmer while stirring constantly until the rice absorbs the stock. Continue to stir and taste, adding stock a cup at a time until the rice is al dente. Finish with the butter and tomato leaf juice or puree.

To serve:

Spoon onto plates. Top each plate with a half cup of the room temperature marinated tomatoes, 2–4 ounces burrata, basil, and a sprinkling of sea salt.

Joan Arnold Farm

Rudolph, Wisconsin

When Joan Arnold looks back on her childhood, she remembers the raspberries. They grew rampant on her family's homestead, where her great-grandparents had established a dairy farm in 1870. During peak season, as the sun shone overhead, she'd take a crate of wooden quarts out to the yard and pick berries while dreaming about what she wanted to do with her life. The plans varied, and some dreams took her on adventures far from home. But in the end, she knew, deep down, that she loved the farm and she'd make her way back to it someday.

Ultimately, that's what she did. She attended college with help from the ROTC program, became a second lieutenant, and spent twenty-eight and a half years in the army. In 2004, she purchased the homestead and 170 acres of the farm from her brother, who also retained 130 acres and his legacy U-pick strawberry operation. When Joan retired in 2007, she moved back to the farm.

From there, she established the Joan Arnold Farm, which she operates using sustainable practices, including companion planting, crop rotation, and composting, with minimal organic inputs used when necessary. Crops include garlic, onions, winter squash, sweet potatoes, and perennials including raspberries, blueberries, and heritage apples. Joan also grows crops like heirloom and cherry tomatoes using high tunnels to control growing conditions and extend the growing season.

From the beginning, Joan has sold her produce, as well as homemade jams, jellies, and salsas, at the Stevens Point Farmers Market. In the early years, she also went door to door to local restaurants, asking whether they were interested in using her produce. It was an exercise that paid off in regular customers, some of whom would make weekly trips to the market for fresh produce. A small cadre have also become loyal buyers who come to the farm's rescue during the peak season when perishable crops like heirloom tomatoes and raspberries are bountiful.

Joan says she appreciates the creativity that local bakeries and restaurants like Main Grain Bakery and Ruby Coffee Roasters employ in using her produce, and she makes a point of paying them a visit during the summer months to try out the dishes they're making with her produce. It's among a series of little rewards she finds amid her daily chores.

After fifteen years of farming, Joan says she still enjoys the physical labor involved in planting her crops, which provides her with plenty of time to think. These days, she plants her onions one by one. It's a monotonous task but one she loves because it offers her a challenge: the sooner they're planted and the better they're weeded, the larger the bulbs will grow. It's just another way of keeping her family farm's 150-plus-year heritage alive.

Cremini Mushroom Risotto with Delicata Squash, Bacon, and Parmesan

Chef David Lynch, Ruby Cafe
with produce from Joan Arnold Farm and bacon from
Liberation Farmers

Ruby Cafe adds a Midwestern twist to this Italian classic by incorporating squash from Joan Arnold Farm and bacon from Liberation Farmers, along with award-winning cheese from Sartori Cheese in Plymouth, Wisconsin. Like any risotto, this recipe is a labor of love that involves time, tasting, and adjustments. But it's well worth your time and effort. It's likely to become a dish you can't wait to make and serve again and again. The risotto pairs well with a dry white wine to counter its richness.

SERVES 5-6

For the squash:

2 medium delicata squash, seeded and cut into half-moon shapes

2 tablespoons olive oil

kosher salt and pepper, to taste

For the risotto:

6-8 cups of chicken or vegetable stock

8 tablespoons olive oil

1 large shallot, minced

4 garlic cloves, minced

1 tablespoon thyme

4 cups cremini mushrooms, sliced

2 cups Arborio rice

1 cup dry white wine. (Chardonnay or Sauvignon blanc)

1 cup heavy cream

To prepare the squash:

Preheat the oven to 350°F.

Toss squash in olive oil and season with salt and pepper. Roast on a large sheet pan in the oven until soft and golden brown, approximately 25 minutes.

To prepare the risotto:

In a stock pot, heat chicken stock to a simmer. Meanwhile, in a different large pot, add olive oil, shallots, garlic, thyme, and mushrooms and sweat over medium heat. Once shallots are translucent, add dry Arborio rice and stir until you begin to hear rice crackle. Add white wine and stir until the wine has all but evaporated. Next, using a ladle, add about one or two cups of heated stock to the rice mixture. Stir frequently until liquid has been absorbed. Continue to add stock in small amounts, stirring until liquid is absorbed. Continue this step until rice is al dente with no remaining liquid in the pot. Finally, reduce heat to low and add heavy cream. Risotto should have the consistency of a viscous liquid. If it is too stiff, additional stock (or more heavy cream) may be added.

For topping:

8 strips bacon, cooked and cut into one-inch squares

1 cup Parmesan, shaved

3 tablespoons fresh parsley, chopped for garnish

To serve:

Spoon risotto into bowls and top with bacon, roasted squash, and shaved Parmesan. Garnish with chopped parsley.

Sassy Cow Creamery

Columbus, Wisconsin
sassycowcreamery.com

Sassy Cow Creamery comprises two family farms situated on 1,700 acres of pastureland. The farms are owned and operated by third-generation farmers James and Robert Baerwolf on land originally purchased by their grandfather in 1946. Farmed by their parents before them and passed down to them in the 1990s, Sassy Cow currently houses both a traditional six-hundred-cow dairy farm operated by Robert and a 250-head organic farm and creamery operated by James. All of the milk and ice cream produced under the Sassy Cow moniker is produced from cows raised on their farms.

SASSY COW CREAMERY

Both Robert and James are graduates of the University of Wisconsin–Madison who began farming when they graduated from college. Over time, farm operations were gradually transferred to them from their parents. By 1999, the original herd of cows were transitioned to Robert's farm, a few miles down the road from the original farm. Today, this is Sassy Cow's traditional dairy, where the cows are housed in a large free-stall barn and can go outside in nice weather.

As interest in organic dairy increased, James took a small group of calves and transitioned them to his organic farm, where he began milking in 2001. For a few years, both farms sold their milk to larger dairy processing plants until they could build the creamery in 2008. This arrangement allowed them to assert more control over both production and pricing for their milk. When the creamery was built on the original family farm, Robert and James adopted the name Sassy Cow Creamery as a means of gaining recognition as a small farmstead dairy.

At that point, they began selling their milk to grocery stores, producing bottled milk, heavy cream, and half-and-half for distribution in Madison, Milwaukee, and Minneapolis and eventually Chicago. In 2008, they launched their own line of premium farmstead ice cream, selling to both grocers and small ice cream shops in Wisconsin. The creamery also sells to restaurants and coffee shops, backing up the work of distributors with follow-up sales calls to ensure their customers are satisfied with the products they receive.

Over a decade later, the work that went into creating Sassy Cow Creamery has paid off, though the creamery's production is still very small in comparison to larger dairies.

Public tours of the farm are available for families and groups who wish to know more about how a dairy farm operates. Guests can also visit the creamery store, which is open seven days a week. On weekdays, customers can view milk being bottled through large viewing windows while purchasing Sassy Cow products, along with cheese, eggs, chocolates, and other Wisconsin-made products. Guests can also order lunches like grilled cheese sandwiches and enjoy housemade Sassy Cow ice cream in the form of cones, dishes, sundaes, shakes, or malts.

Honeypie Cafe's Wisconsin Cheese and Macaroni

Chef and managing partner Derek Petersen, Honeypie Cafe with cream from Sassy Cow Creamery

If you've been searching for creamy, indulgent homemade macaroni and cheese, consider your goal reached. This fantastic rendition from Honeypie Cafe is rich and flavorful thanks to amazing Sassy Cow Creamery cream and superior Wisconsin Carr Valley cheeses. It takes a bit of time, but it's worth every second.

LORI FREDRICH

SERVES 4-6

- 4 cups heavy cream
- 2 cups shredded three-year aged cheddar, divided
- 2 cups shredded baby cheddar, divided
- 16 ounces high-quality elbow macaroni
- ½ cup salted butter, melted
- 1 cup panko breadcrumbs
- ½ cup grated Parmesan
- 1 cup cooked, chopped bacon
- ½ cup sliced scallions

Preheat the oven to 400°F.

Simmer heavy cream on medium-low for 45 minutes until it starts to thicken. Add 1 cup of aged and 1 cup baby cheddar and whisk until smooth.

While the heavy cream is simmering, bring water to a boil in a 6–8-quart pot and cook the macaroni for 8–10 minutes or until al dente. Strain the pasta and fold into the cheese sauce.

Grease a casserole dish well and spoon the pasta and cheese mixture inside. Top with the remaining cheddar cheese. Cover with foil and bake for 45 minutes. Mix the melted butter and panko breadcrumbs together. Remove the tin foil and spread the buttered breadcrumbs and grated Parmesan on top of the macaroni and cheese. Broil for 2 minutes. Remove from the oven and top with bacon and scallions before serving.

Wild Mushroom and Mascarpone Tortelli in Parmesan Broth

Executive Chef Dustin Urbanik, Grand Geneva Resort & Spa
with mushrooms from River Valley Ranch

Grand Geneva Resort sources phenomenal hen of the woods and shiitake mushrooms from River Valley Ranch. At Ristorantè Brissago, the chefs roast the mushrooms in the resort's 800-degree wood oven. From there, they are finely minced and folded into an indulgent pasta filling made with Pecorino Romano and mascarpone cheeses. The dish is finished with sweet onion velvet, tarragon-infused butter, roasted local corn, and red-veined sorrel leaves from Creator Farms in Burlington.

In this simplified version, rich mushroom and mascarpone tortelli are served in a rich Parmesan broth and topped with onion velvet and Parmesan cheese. Feel free to add roasted sweet corn, sautéed spinach, or other seasonal ingredients to make it your own.

For the Parmesan broth:

1 tablespoon neutral oil (grapeseed or canola)

1 carrot, peeled and diced

2 celery stalks, diced

4 garlic cloves, smashed

½ cup dry white wine

1 bay leaf

4 sprigs fresh thyme

8 ounces Parmesan rind, left over from other uses

32 ounces water

heavy cream (optional)

For the pasta dough:

1 pound 00 flour

4 eggs

½ tablespoon extra virgin olive oil

½ teaspoon kosher salt

To prepare the Parmesan broth:

Place oil in a medium stock pot over medium heat; add the carrot, celery, and garlic, and sauté them until they are aromatic. Add the white wine and reduce it to one-eighth of the volume. Add the remaining ingredients, reduce heat to low, and simmer the broth for one hour. Run the stock through a strainer or colander into a clean bowl. The broth can be made ahead and stored in the refrigerator.

Note: When you reheat the Parmesan broth, you can add a small amount of heavy cream and cook it for a few minutes longer if you'd prefer a broth with slightly more body.

To prepare the dough:

Mound the flour on a clean prep area and make a well in the middle of the flour. With a fork, start with one egg at a time and incorporate the eggs into the flour. Halfway through, slowly drizzle the extra virgin olive oil and salt in the dough. Once all the eggs are incorporated, knead the dough for 5 minutes to develop the gluten. This process will result in a soft, velvety pasta dough. Let the dough rest for 30–45 minutes under a damp towel. While the pasta is resting, you can prepare the pasta filling and onion velvet.

For the mushrooms:

2 tablespoons butter

5 sprigs fresh thyme, minced

1 sprig fresh rosemary, minced

1 pound hen of the woods mushrooms

1 pound shiitake mushrooms

½ shallot, finely minced

2 garlic cloves, finely minced

2 tablespoons dry white wine

kosher salt and black pepper

For the tortelli filling:

prepared mushrooms (from above)

4 cups mascarpone cheese

1 Meyer lemon, juiced and zested

½ tablespoon fennel pollen

1 garlic clove, minced

kosher salt, to taste

For the onion velvet:

1 tablespoon choice of neutral oil

2 sweet onions, Vidalia, Walla Walla, or other favorite variety, julienned

1 tablespoon honey

zest and juice from ¼ of a Meyer lemon

kosher salt, to taste

For the garnish:

shaved Parmesan

To prepare the mushrooms:

Using a clean, medium-size, and heavy-bottomed sauté pan, melt the butter with the thyme and rosemary over low heat. Add the mushrooms and turn the heat up to medium. During this step, let the mushrooms cook without too much stirring. It will help to caramelize the mushrooms and give them color and flavor in the end product. Add shallots, garlic, wine, and seasoning, and stir until shallots are translucent. If the pan looks dry, add more oil, a teaspoon at a time. Mushrooms should be golden brown and buttery with an herbal finish. Set the mushrooms aside until you make the tortelli filling. Reserve some mushrooms for garnishing the final dish.

To prepare the filling:

Finely dice the sautéed mushrooms. Place in a clean mixing bowl and fold in the mascarpone, lemon juice and zest, fennel pollen, and minced garlic until well incorporated. Season with salt to taste.

To prepare the onion velvet:

Begin with a clean sauté pan over low heat; add oil and onions. Cook the onions, stirring occasionally until they develop a deep golden brown color. If your pan seems dry, you can add a teaspoon of water to keep the onions from burning. Add honey, lemon zest, and the juice, and cook on low for five minutes. Cool the onions and transfer to a blender and puree until a smooth texture is achieved. Season with kosher salt to your liking. Set aside for plating the dish.

To fill the pasta:

While you fill the pasta, bring a medium pot of salted water to a boil.

Using a pasta roller, start on the thickest setting and continue to run the dough through until it has been run through the thinnest setting. This result can also be achieved using a rolling pin.

Then place tablespoons of tortelli filling on one of the long sides of the pasta dough, spacing each spoonful of filling 1 inch apart and far enough from the edge of the dough to allow for sealing the pasta. Repeat this step until you run out of filling or you have reached the number of tortelli you'd like to make.

When you've placed all of your filling on the dough, fold the dough over the filling and trim any excess pasta from the edges. Using your hands or a fork, gently press down on the space in between the filling to create a seal. Cut out tortellis using a pasta cutter or sharp knife.

Drop tortelli into the seasoned water and cook for 5 minutes or until tortellis rise to the top.

To serve:

Place the tortelli in a bowl and pour the Parmesan broth over the top. Garnish with reserved mushrooms, onion velvet, and shaved Parmesan.

Rushing Waters Fisheries

Palmyra, Wisconsin
rushingwaters.net

The largest rainbow trout farm in Wisconsin can be found on eighty acres of glaciated land in southeast Wisconsin's Kettle Moraine State Forest.

Prior to World War II, the land—which boasts picturesque hills and valleys—was home to a fur farm where foxes were raised and their pelts sold to furriers in Europe and Hong Kong. But starting in the 1940s, trout became the focus. Ponds on the property were stocked with trout, which were then sold at nearby ports, including Navy Pier in Chicago.

RUSHING WATERS FISHERIES

But the Rushing Waters that exists today began in 1994 when Bill Graham purchased the farm with the intention of making Rushing Waters a leader in modern aquaculture. By 1997, he'd hired Peter Fritsch, a young limnologist who'd just completed his degree at the University of Wisconsin–Stevens Point. Together, they refocused their efforts on the quality of the water and the feed for their fish. That meant no shortcuts and no chemicals.

The rainbow trout at Rushing Waters are raised in fifty-six ponds on the property. The ponds themselves are man-made, but they're fed by water from springs and artesian wells. Throughout their life cycles, the trout are grown in a natural environment, complete with sunshine, weeds, and bugs. It's an environment that offers multiple benefits over indoor aquaculture, first and foremost because it promotes the health and well-being of the fish, which lives out its life much as it would in the wild.

To ensure that their fish are harvested, cleaned, and packaged as fresh as possible, Rushing Waters operates an on-site FDA/HACCP (Hazard Analysis Critical Control Point)-certified production facility where the trout are processed. The facility also manufactures a number of additional seafood products, including smoked fish, wild Alaskan salmon burgers, seafood spreads, and crabcakes. Freshly frozen fish and other products can be purchased directly from Rushing Waters at their farm store, with about 75 percent of their stock sold to grocers and retail stores across the state.

For many years, the farm provided fish to restaurants across the country, from the French Laundry to Rick Bayless's Topolobampo and Frontera Grill. But when the nation and its restaurants turned their focus to locally sourced proteins and produce in 2002, the market shifted. Today, Rushing Waters trout is found in retail stores primarily throughout the Midwest. Today the fishery services mostly Wisconsin restaurants, processing and delivering the fish within 24 hours of harvest.

Year-round, visitors are welcome to tour the ecofriendly fish farm. The public is also invited to try their hands at catching fish from Rushing Waters's public fishing pond. Fishing poles, bait, and buckets are provided. Guests just pay for the fish they catch.

Grilled Trout with Armenian Green Bean and Tomato Stew

Chef Justin Aprahamian, Sanford
with trout from Rushing Waters Fisheries

Seasonally driven dishes define the menu at Sanford, but global inflection is also a showpiece. Dishes like this stew are an intimate reflection of Chef Justin Aprahamian's Armenian heritage and cuisine, which typically relies more heavily on the quality and freshness of ingredients than the liberal use of spices. That tendency is evident here in the preparation of the trout, which is simply seasoned and grilled, as well as the comforting vegetable stew, which provides the backbone for the dish.

SERVES 6

For the stew:

12 ounces fresh green beans, blanched

12 ounces onion, diced small

4 tablespoons extra virgin olive oil, plus 1 tablespoon for serving

1 teaspoon garlic, minced

½ teaspoon fennel

1 teaspoon dried tarragon

¾ cup white wine

1 pound tomatoes, medium diced (or a 28 oz. can of good-quality whole tomatoes, drained and diced)

salt and pepper, to taste

For the trout:

3 whole trout, scaled, filleted, with pin bones removed

kosher salt

black pepper

extra virgin olive oil

To prepare the stew:

Prepare an ice bath. Bring a pot of salted water to a boil. Place green beans in the boiling water for 30 seconds, or until just tender, and then place immediately into the ice bath to stop the cooking. Once chilled, remove from ice bath and cut into ½-inch pieces on a bias. Set aside.

In a saucepan, sweat onions in olive oil over medium heat until translucent and tender, but not caramelized (about 3–5 minutes). Add garlic, fennel, and tarragon and cook until fragrant—about 2 minutes more. Add white wine and reduce by about two-thirds. Add diced tomatoes and slowly raise the heat. Cook 3–5 minutes to incorporate, and season with salt and pepper to taste. If making ahead, chill and keep separate from green beans.

When ready to serve, gently warm tomato mixture, add green beans and 1 tablespoon extra virgin olive oil, and warm through. Adjust seasoning as necessary.

To prepare the fish:

While the green beans are warming, cook the trout on a very hot grill. Cook the trout most of the way on the skin side to crisp it up and just finish it on the meat side. Season the trout to taste with salt and ground black pepper. Drizzle a bit of olive oil on the skin of the trout, as doing so will add some flavor and help prevent the skin from sticking to the grill. Grill about 2 minutes on the skin side (a little more or less depending on the heat of the grill)

and turn the fish over. The meat side will cook very quickly (less than a minute). Remove from grill and serve over green bean and tomato stew. Good accompaniments for this dish would be some roasted fingerling potatoes and a fresh sorrel salad.

Seared Whitefish with Taktouka

The chef team at Trixie's
with produce from the Wickman House Garden

Morocco meets the Midwest in this flavorful dish that combines Lake Michigan white fish with farm-fresh bell peppers and warming spices. With the exception of the spice blends, all ingredients can be procured locally in Wisconsin in mid- to late summer.

For the rice:

1 cup cooked Wisconsin grown wild rice, or best available local grain

2 teaspoons grapeseed oil

½ onion, diced

2–3 garlic cloves, minced

1 teaspoon smoked sweet paprika

1 teaspoon chipotle powder

1 teaspoon dark chili powder

1 cup white wine

½ cup tomato paste

1 quart mushroom or vegetable stock

1 tablespoon butter

1 tablespoon garlic, minced

1 teaspoon fresh lemon juice

For the taktouka:

4 tablespoons grapeseed oil

1 onion, julienned

5–7 garlic cloves, or one head of garlic, minced

2 teaspoons toasted and ground cumin, or to taste

2 teaspoons black pepper, or to taste

2 teaspoons coriander, or to taste

2 red bell peppers, seeds and stem removed, julienned

2 yellow bell peppers, seeds and stem removed, julienned

kosher salt, to taste

4 cups high-quality local roasted red peppers, stems and seeds removed, diced

½ cup champagne vinegar

6 cups high-quality oven-roasted local heirloom tomatoes, whole, skins removed

For the hawaij spice blend:

8 tablespoons high-quality cocoa powder

2 tablespoons ground black pepper

2 tablespoons ground turmeric

2 tablespoons ground cardamom

2 tablespoons ground cumin

For the whitefish:

1 Lake Michigan whitefish fillet, skinned and divided into halves

kosher salt

hawaij spice blend

4 tablespoons grapeseed oil

For the salad:

¼ cup finely shredded local napa cabbage

¼ cup high-quality local greens, such as field greens or arugula

¼ cup kale or collards, julienned

¼ cup frisée or mustard greens

1 pinch of candied lemon peel

5–8 whole mint leaves

1 teaspoon minced chives

2 teaspoons high-quality extra virgin olive oil

2 teaspoons lemon juice

pinch of salt, to taste

For the garnish:

extra virgin olive oil

cacao nibs

fresh chives

mint leaves

To prepare the rice:

Cook rice (or grain of choice) and reserve.

In a stock pot, sauté onions and minced garlic in about 2 teaspoons of grapeseed oil or other high-temperature cooking oil over medium heat. When onions and garlic are fragrant and just beginning to caramelize, add the paprika, chipotle powder, and dark chili powder. Stir continuously into the garlic and onion to bloom spices (about 30 seconds). Add the white wine and tomato paste, stirring to combine. Allow the mixture to cook down and thicken, stirring occasionally. Keep a close eye on it, as the mixture can burn easily.

Add the mushroom or vegetable stock to the spices and alliums and bring to a boil.

Reduce heat and simmer the seasoned stock for 10–15 minutes, and then strain through a fine mesh sieve. This process yields more seasoned stock than needed for the recipe. Store the remaining stock in an airtight container in the refrigerator and use within a week.

Just before cooking the whitefish, sauté 1 tablespoon of minced garlic in a pan with 1 tablespoon of butter. When butter begins to lightly brown, add the cooked rice, ⅓ cup of the seasoned mushroom or vegetable stock, and 1 teaspoon of lemon juice. Sauté or stir until the rice is heated through.

To prepare the taktouka:

In a large, wide-bottomed pan, sweat onions and garlic in grapeseed oil over medium heat until fragrant. Add the ground spices and stir continuously to bloom (about 30 seconds). Add the julienned bell peppers and season to taste with salt. Reduce the heat to medium and allow the fresh vegetables to begin to cook down (about 10 minutes). If the pan becomes too dry and the vegetables stick, deglaze with a little stock or water.

Add the diced roasted peppers and all accompanying juices, plus the champagne vinegar, and continue to cook for 5–10 more minutes before adding the roasted heirloom tomatoes. Bring the pan back to a boil and then reduce to a simmer until the liquid begins to cook down and the taktouka starts to thicken to a curry-like texture. Continue to mash the taktouka with a wooden spoon during the cooking process to help break down the vegetables. Taste the taktouka and adjust the flavor, adding additional champagne vinegar, salt, and spices to your liking. Keep the taktouka warm while you prepare the fish.

To prepare the hawaij spice blend:

Thoroughly blend all the ingredients. Hawaij blend will yield more than needed for the recipe. Store in an airtight glass jar for up to 6 months.

To prepare the whitefish:

Season both sides of the whitefish with salt and the hawaij seasoning blend. Heat 4 tablespoons of grapeseed oil in a large heavy skillet over medium-high heat. Place fish in the pan gently, skin-side up, and sear until the flesh is golden and lifts easily from the pan (about 3 minutes). When one side of the fish is seared, remove from heat, flip to uncooked side, and let rest for 30 seconds in the pan before removing it.

At this point, mix all of the salad ingredients together in a large bowl and set aside.

To plate the dish:

Place rice in a shallow bowl. Spoon 1 cup of the cooked taktouka on top of the rice and place the seared whitefish fillets on top of the taktouka, stacking one fillet on top of the other. Balance a generous pile of the seasoned salad greens on top of the whitefish and garnish with a drizzle of high-quality extra virgin olive oil, a sprinkle of cacao nibs, chives, and mint leaves (or other fresh herbs from the garden).

Roots & Stems

Mequon, Wisconsin
rstems.com

Pick any day in midsummer as twilight falls over the fields at Roots & Stems farm. It wouldn't be out of the ordinary to see a child flitting across a field of flowers chasing fireflies as the sun sinks slowly below the horizon.

Experiencing nature was something that Brenda and Steve Schieble wanted for their children, and it was part of their reasoning for purchasing the farm where they now reside. Brenda had grown up on a hobby farm. It was a lifestyle she says she grew to appreciate, and one she aspired to emulate as she started her own family.

After years of searching, Brenda and Steve found the eighteen-acre property where they would settle down. Although there was a great deal of work involved in rehabilitating the house and barn, the couple saw the potential around them and were inspired to put in the work necessary to help the farm reach its full potential.

At the time, Brenda was working as a commercial interior designer, but she also had an enjoyable side gig working for Witte's Vegetable Farm in Cedarburg. As it turns out, her job at Witte's would serve as inspiration for launching Roots & Stems.

In 2018, Roots & Stems planted their first crop: garlic. It was not only a crop with plentiful health benefits but also one with growing consumer demand, especially at local marketplaces like Witte's. As an added benefit, they knew they could grow it without the assistance of pesticides or chemicals. The following year, they added cut flowers to the mix.

Brenda had originally begun planting flowers with the goal of creating a cutting garden during her maternity leave. She grew a fairly wide variety to cut for the house and began sharing the wealth with friends and neighbors. When she found she had enough, she sold some to Witte's, and they took off. By 2019, Roots & Stems built a greenhouse where Brenda could propagate more flowers.

Today, the farm boasts eight acres of flowers, including a sunflower path, and produces thousands of pounds of hardneck garlic (plus spring garlic scapes) annually. Both are sold through Witte's, as well as at other local farmers markets. Roots & Stems also offers a you-pick option for customers right at the farm.

Brenda says it's been so rewarding to watch people as they venture into the fields to gather flowers, to breathe, and to experience the peace that comes from spending time outdoors.

They've entered the hospitality realm somewhat cautiously, connecting with restaurants and food trucks primarily through word of mouth and offering venues the opportunity to try out different varieties of garlic to discover what they like and what they'd like to continue buying. Ultimately, the needs and wants of local restaurants could assist in shaping the future of the farm.

Kukhura Choyla

Chef Barkha Limbu Daily, the cheel
with garlic from Roots & Stems

A traditional dish among people in the Kathmandu Valley in Nepal, kukhura choyla typically relies on water buffalo for its main protein. But the recipe is highly adaptable and can be made with beef, buffalo, pork, or even dry toasted soybeans. Here, it's made with boneless, skinless chicken thighs. In Chef Barkha Limbu Daily's hometown of Kathmandu, the dish is traditionally served at room temperature. It's most often accompanied by flattened rice, but it's equally delicious on its own or served with steamed rice.

THE CHEEL

For the marinade:

2 pounds boneless, skinless chicken thighs

kosher salt

1 tablespoon oil (vegetable oil or olive oil)

1 tablespoon cumin

1 tablespoon coriander

1 tablespoon garlic paste

1 tablespoon ginger paste

For the chicken:

1 tablespoon ginger, julienned

1 tablespoon garlic, julienned

½ cup onions, julienned

2 tablespoons serrano peppers, julienned (optional for heat)

1 tablespoon fresh squeezed lemon juice, to taste

¼ teaspoon ground Nepalese Szechuan pepper (substitute black pepper or Chinese Szechuan pepper)

1 teaspoon paprika

1 teaspoon mustard oil

1 teaspoon fenugreek

½ teaspoon turmeric

½ teaspoon ground Nepalese red pepper (substitute cayenne pepper) (optional for heat)

2 tablespoons cilantro, chopped

To prepare the chicken with marinade:

Salt and oil the chicken thighs. In a small pan over medium-high heat, dry roast the cumin and coriander, and then grind in a spice grinder. Combine garlic paste, ginger paste, toasted cumin, and coriander, and rub on chicken thighs. Cover and refrigerate overnight (or at least a few hours).

To prepare the chicken:

Grill both sides of the chicken until cooked; use oven if needed to reach 165°F internal temperature. Remove and allow to cool. Cut all chicken into ½-inch cubes.

In a bowl, mix the chicken, ginger, garlic, onion, serrano peppers, lemon juice, Szechuan pepper, and paprika. In a pan, add the mustard oil and the fenugreek. Toast until the fenugreek seed turns dark. Add the turmeric and red pepper, and immediately remove from the heat. Temper the spices by gradually adding a spoonful of the chicken mixture, stirring the pan until everything is thoroughly combined. Top it all off with chopped cilantro when ready to serve.

Serve on its own or with rice.

ROOTS & STEMS

Milwaukee Microgreens

Milwaukee, Wisconsin
milwaukeemicrogreens.com

It was fall of 2018 when Patrick Darrough began experimenting with microgreens, growing them in a spare bedroom at his home. His interest in urban agriculture had been piqued after he chose to leave a joyless corporate sales job, and he'd spent a fair amount of time educating himself and making connections across the urban farming landscape. When a hopeful position with Growing Power didn't pan out, he decided to take matters into his own hands.

In January 2019, he took the leap, partnering with Shannon Dunne and Erik Bergstrom, two close friends who'd also left corporate America in pursuit of a higher calling. Together, the partners launched Milwaukee Microgreens, an urban farm that produces fresh, locally grown microgreens. Their goal? Create a new brand of urban farming that provides urban dwellers with food that's both fresh and high in nutrition.

Nearly simultaneously, Erik, Shannon, and Patrick decided to launch Milwaukee Farmers United (MFU), an online farmers market offering free local delivery of farm-fresh produce and locally made food products to homes in the greater Milwaukee area. Ultimately, the two businesses would work in tandem to provide consumers affordable, easy-to-access locally grown food, connect eaters and producers in a meaningful way, and contribute to the growth of the local economy.

Both businesses were founded in a suburban warehouse space in Menomonee Falls. But business took off quickly, and by 2020 the partners needed to relocate to a larger nineteen-hundred-square-foot warehouse space in Milwaukee's Bay View neighborhood.

Using a soil mix of peat moss, coconut coir, perlite, and organic nutrients, plus high-efficiency LED lighting, Milwaukee Microgreens grows up to 125 pounds of microgreens a week with a selection of over thirty varieties grown over the course of a year. Regular offerings include fifteen staple varieties, plus a rotating selection of specialty micros, including

cantaloupe, parsley, beets, fennel, carrots, sage, chervil, and amaranth.

It's the versatility of the tiny but nutrient-dense microgreens—which can be grown from almost any type of seed—that provides daily inspiration for the Milwaukee Microgreens crew. Pushing the envelope, trying new things, and educating the public about the virtues of adding microgreens to their everyday diets are all part of an average day's work.

But logistics are also part of running a successful operation. As they established the business, the partners spent a great deal of time prospecting for restaurant business. They spent an equal amount of time rethinking the farm–customer relationship, including how their relationships with restaurants would be structured. The goal was to offer a product that was not only local but also fresh and easy to obtain.

For that reason, sending restaurants a fresh list every week didn't make sense. Microgreens grow on a schedule, taking about ten days to reach maturity. When they reach their peak, they are beautifully fresh but also highly perishable. So establishing a system based on standing orders became the norm.

Today, Milwaukee Microgreens maintains a core list of between twenty and forty restaurants they service throughout the year, along with a few catering companies and private chefs. Most are regular clients, and new business nearly always comes via word of mouth.

When asked what drives them forward, the partners are quick to answer. They consider it an honor to grow nutritious food in and for the community on a year-round basis. They view nourishing the public as a privilege and are proud to know that their day-to-day grind is an integral part of Milwaukee's budding local food revolution.

Chicken Korma

Abhishek Patil, Saffron Modern Indian Dining
with microgreens from Milwaukee Microgreens

Bold flavors are a signature at Saffron, which melds traditional Indian fare with modern elements and locally sourced ingredients. You'll find that full flavor in this classic chicken korma, which harnesses the flavors of warming Indian spices in a yogurt-based masala curry. Note that the chefs at Saffron also make brilliant use of the microgreens from Milwaukee Microgreens, harnessing both their concentrated flavor and nutritional content by using them as an ingredient, as well as a garnish.

Serve this dish with warm na'an or steamed basmati rice.

SAFFRON

SERVES 4

5 tablespoons olive oil

1 tablespoon cumin seeds

1-inch knob of ginger, chopped finely

5–6 cloves garlic, chopped finely

1½ red onion, sliced

2¾ cups tomato puree

1 cup whole milk plain yogurt

½ teaspoon turmeric

½ teaspoon coriander powder

½ teaspoon paprika (add an extra ½ teaspoon for extra spice)

½ teaspoon fenugreek (if using dried, pinch between your fingers to break up)

8–9 ounces (about 1 cup) bone-in chicken, chopped

2 ounces spicy microgreens, divided

½ cup heavy cream

½ cup unsalted butter, cubed

kosher salt

1 ounce micro cilantro (or chopped cilantro leaves)

Add olive oil to a large pan on low to medium heat. Once oil has been heating for a couple of minutes, add the cumin seeds and cook 1–2 minutes or until fragrant. If the heat is too high, the cumin seeds will burn.

Lower the heat and add ginger and garlic; cook 2–3 minutes on low heat. Add sliced onions and sauté 3–4 minutes until golden brown. Add tomato puree and cook together for another 6–8 minutes or until you see the puree reducing and darkening in color.

Slowly mix in yogurt. Once yogurt is well mixed, add in spices. Cook spices until oil starts to disappear. Add chicken and cook for 10 minutes until juices run clear. Once chicken is cooked through, add 1 ounce of spicy blend microgreens. When microgreens have wilted, add cream and butter. Let this cook for another 4–5 minutes on low-medium heat. Season with salt to taste.

Garnish with the rest of the micro spicy blend and micro cilantro.

Vitruvian Farms

McFarland, Wisconsin
vitruvianfarms.com

When Tommy Stauffer and Shawn Kuhn started their six-acre farm in 2010, their main focus was to relocalize the food system. The movement at the time was not nearly as well established as it is now, so their goal was to contribute to a vibrant local food economy, connect people to the food that they were eating, and revitalize the farming industry by providing not only seasonal jobs but also full-time jobs in agriculture. They wanted to see farming used as a driver in the repair of our ecosystem and food as a vehicle for community improvement.

Neither had grown up on a farm. Shawn was a philosophy major who wanted to change the world, and Tommy was a business major who found himself torn between using his education to make money or to do something more meaningful. Eventually, it was Shawn's passion and hope for change that drew him into the agricultural fray.

You might be wondering what it means to be vitruvian. Perhaps you recognize the *Vitruvian Man*, a drawing by Leonardo da Vinci. Shawn and Tommy named the farm for Vitruvius, a Roman architect, engineer, and writer who lived during the first century BCE. He believed all human endeavors should aim to encompass the values of balance and beauty. So when the two set out to build their farm, they did so with the goal of

VITRUVIAN FARMS

crafting a place of beauty, a place where the landscape operated in balance with nature—and where they could nurture their community with food.

The two began with a garden filled with salad, which they sold at a local Madison market. That first sale gave them confidence and drove them to focus on how to grow better, grow more. It was their drive to produce consistent greens that moved them forward, leading to the addition of microgreens and mushrooms, along with seven greenhouses. Today, they operate a certified organic vegetable farm, community-supported agriculture (CSA) program, and farm market for which they produce greenhouses of tomatoes, peppers, carrots, beets, and turnips.

It was restaurants, though, that drove the growth of the farm. Shawn and Tommy committed to the goal of making it easy for eateries to get what they needed, meeting with chefs during the winter months to gather inspiration for things to grow and cultivating relationships throughout the area. Today, their produce is on plates in over forty Madison restaurants, and they have a collection of chefs they can put on "speed dial" when they need someone to purchase an overabundance of unique CSA vegetables during peak season. They are also a major supplier of produce for Madison's Willy Street Cooperative.

Despite the work (which both partners admit is exhausting and far from glamorous), Shawn and Tommy developed an immense love for food over the past decade. Their appreciation doesn't necessarily stem from a culinary perspective, but the experience of witnessing the miraculous process of taking a seed, planting it, nurturing it, and being able to pick it and eat it right there has become both an inspiration and a driver for the work they do every single day.

Mushroom and Swiss Bratwurst

Chef Daniel Fox, Heritage Tavern
with mushrooms from Vitruvian Farms

*Traditional German bratwurst is taken up a notch with the addition of earthy shii-
take mushrooms and nutty Swiss cheese in this recipe from Chef Daniel Fox. Serve
the cooked sausage with his Bacon-Braised Cabbage and Sour Cream Spaetzle (see
pages 90 and 96). The sausages are also delicious alongside roasted potatoes.*

*This recipe makes enough sausages to warrant a sausage-making party. Divide
the work among friends and let everyone take home a portion of the sausages. Any
sausages you cannot use right away should keep for at least two to three months in
the freezer.*

*Note: High-temp cheese has a 400° melting point, making it ideal for use in
sausages, as it's less likely to leak out of the casings. You can ask for high-temp
cheese at any reputable cheese shop. This recipe uses Swiss cheese, but you can use
another high-temp cheese if you'd prefer.*

MAKES 36–40 SAUSAGES

1 pound shiitake
  mushrooms

10 pounds pork shoulder

1 cup water, ice cold

½ pound high-temp
  Swiss cheese, grated
  or cut into a small dice

¼ cup kosher salt

1 tablespoon plus
  1 teaspoon granulated
  garlic

2 teaspoon coriander

2 teaspoon black
  peppercorn

1 teaspoon marjoram

1 teaspoon cumin

1 teaspoon chili powder

¼ cup Madeira (optional)

natural hog casings

Preheat the oven to 275°F.

It is very important to keep all ingredients and equipment as
cold as possible during sausage production. Place attach-
ments of the grinder in the freezer to chill well before use.

To prepare the mushrooms, destem and cut into ¼-inch
strips. Roast the mushrooms in the preheated 275°F oven for
1 hour or until lightly caramelized and dry to the touch. Cut
the pork shoulder into long thin strips. The strips of meat
should fit into the tube of the grinder with little effort. Partially freeze strips of pork before grinding. Grind the strips
of meat through a ¼-inch grinder die two times. The second
time the meat is run through the grinder, incorporate the ice
water gradually. Place the pork in a large bowl with another
bowl filled partially with ice underneath. Evenly mix the
cheese, mushrooms, Madeira (if using), and the rest of the
dry ingredients into the ground meat. Mix and fold the mixture for at least 2–3 minutes. It is important to mix all ingredients together very well. An elasticity or emulsion should
develop within the meat.

Flush out the inside of the casings well with cold running
water, and then allow the casings to soak in ice water for
at least 20 minutes, reserving them in the cold water until

Special equipment:

meat grinder,
  sausage stuffing
  tube, sausage prick

ready to use. Slide one casing on a medium sausage stuffing tube, and tie the end of the casing to begin stuffing sausage. Stuff sausage to a medium firmness in the casings. Twist sausage links into 5- or 6-inch links. Prick sausage links as needed with a sausage prick. Let sausage mature in the refrigerator for 24 hours before using or freezing.

When you are ready to prepare the sausages, they can be poached, grilled, or seared. The finished sausage should register an internal temperature of 145°F.

Whitefeather Organics

Custer, Wisconsin
whitefeatherorganics.farm

Tony Whitefeather's passion for the environment was cultivated from an early age. He grew up spending summers with his grandparents, who operated a farm in Door County. The experience stuck with him. By the time he was in his twenties, he found himself asking questions like "Where is the world going?" and "How can I be a part of helping to heal the environment and live in harmony with nature?" In the end, the answer was farming.

Tony spent years working on farms in both the United States and Canada, knocking on farmers' doors and learning everything he could. Then he and his wife, Laura, began shopping for land to call their own. It took them four years, but in 2006 they found thirty acres in Custer, Wisconsin. The land was in rough shape; for years, it had been used for raising dairy cattle and the soil throughout the property's glaciated rolling hills had been depleted of its fertility. But Tony and Laura took that scrappy piece of land and divided it into thirteen fields, planting the hills with native plants to promote pollinators and growing vegetables in the lower fertile areas.

By 2007, they were able to launch a CSA program that remains a foundational element for the farm. The farm has since achieved both Organic and Real Organic certification, under which it grows crops including multiple varieties of potatoes, sweet corn, cauliflower, greens, and tomatoes, along with pastured chickens and pigs and laying hens—all of which benefit from Tony's interest in soil and soil biology and the impact of terroir on flavor.

In addition to CSA shares, Whitefeather Organics sells their produce at local farmers markets, as well as to over fifteen restaurants and small food businesses, including Father Fats, Ruby Coffee Roasters Cafe, Tine & Cellar, Red Eye Brewing Co., and Siren Shrub Co., which uses the farm's flavorful fresh basil to make their basil drinking shrub. Tony says their work with restaurants has offered them an opportunity to showcase the quality of their produce at the hands of talented local chefs; in addition, requests from those chefs have impacted the vegetables they grow on the farm.

Tony is certain that it takes a lifetime to learn how to farm. He admits there are tough days, but the inspiration he draws from the changing seasons and the ability to improve their processes from year to year is what keeps him moving forward. "We built this farm from scratch," he says. "We built all the buildings. When I get up in the morning, I watch my dogs as they scare off the deer. I see the land and the plantings in the three fields closest to the house and I move forward knowing that we've created something for our community that we hope will last far beyond our lifetime."

WHITEFEATHER ORGANICS

Italian Sausage, Kale, and Potato Stew

Chef David Lynch, Ruby Cafe
with potatoes from Whitefeather Organics

This hearty stew is perfect for a cold winter evening snowed in at home, though most of the vegetables are readily available all year long. The beautiful texture of the roasted butterball potatoes from Whitefeather Organics is a highlight in this stew; seek them out if you are able. Also be sure to invest in a good artisan loaf of bread to enjoy with the stew and soak up its delicious broth. Ruby Cafe serves it with bread from Main Grain Bakery in Stevens Point.

SERVES 5-6

For the Italian sausage:

2 pounds of ground pork

1 tablespoon dried fennel seeds

1 tablespoon dried basil

1 tablespoon garlic powder

½ tablespoon onion powder

½ tablespoon red pepper flakes

kosher salt and pepper, to taste

For the stew:

¼ cup olive oil

1 large onion, diced

2 large carrots, diced

2 stalks celery, diced

6 leaves of kale, chopped

4 garlic cloves, minced

6 large butterball potatoes, cut in ¾-inch cubes

2-3 tablespoons olive oil

kosher salt and pepper, to taste

8 cups chicken stock

1 tablespoon dried thyme

3 tablespoon fresh parsley, chopped

5 slices of rustic white bread

To prepare the Italian sausage:

Mix all ingredients by hand or using a kitchen mixer. Place seasoned meat in a large stock pot and cook over medium heat. Once browned, remove meat and set aside. Leave brown fond on the bottom of the pot.

To prepare the stew:

Preheat the oven to 350°F.

In the same stock pot, add olive oil, onions, carrots, celery, kale, and garlic, tossing to combine. Cook over medium heat until tender. Stir occasionally while scraping the bottom of the pot to release the fond.

While the vegetables cook, toss the potatoes in olive oil and season with salt and pepper. Roast in the oven until golden brown, approximately 25 minutes. Add chicken stock and thyme to the stock pot and bring to a boil. Add roasted potatoes and reserved Italian sausage, and simmer for 30-40 minutes. Just before serving, stir in chopped parsley. Serve with rustic bread.

Liberation Farmers

Almond, Wisconsin
liberationfarmers.com

Connections to both the land and the community have been driving forces for John Sheffy and Holly Petrillo, owners of Liberation Farmers, a twenty-four-acre farm in Portage County, Wisconsin.

They began their journeys with backgrounds in natural resource ecology and were both swept up in the local food movement in the early 2000s as they pursued involvement with community-supported agriculture programs and farmers markets. One of the things that attracted them to one another when they met was a common interest in gardening, food, farming, and foraging.

Before purchasing their farm, the couple lived in Stevens Point, where they ran a small urban farm. But they decided they needed more space and more land. So, in 2011, they made the move to their twenty-four-acre farm, where they began to practice permaculture through the establishment of perennial fruit and nut trees, producing annual vegetables (which are grown using no-till methods, crop rotation, and heavy mulching practices), and renting sixteen acres of pastureland as grazing space for animals.

Goats are kept in a winter paddock with a high tunnel that provides shelter for them in the winter. In the spring, the manure they've left behind contributes to the fertility of the soil, which is used to grow tomatoes, eggplants, and peppers. Similarly, as animals feed from large bales of hay during the winter months, they leave behind both waste hay and manure, which is used to mulch the farm's winter squash and pumpkins.

Over time, their interest in sustainable global agriculture led them to work directly with coffee farmers in Mexico and Kenya to purchase coffee, which they roasted and sold along with vegetables, meat, and eggs. To advance their business, in 2018 they purchased a small village grocery store in Almond that they transformed into a café they named Adelante, meaning "forward" in Spanish. There they established a roastery for their coffee along with a place to host farm-to-table taco and pizza nights using locally grown vegetables from the farm.

In addition to supplying their café, Liberation Farmers supplies meats to other local restaurants, including Ruby Cafe and Michelle's Restaurant, all customers who connected with the farm through word of mouth. Each restaurant has its unique set of requests. Some place standing orders; others reach out when they are hosting special events and would like to showcase something special. Chef Cristian of Father Fats Public House and Chef's Kitchen is a particularly avid supporter of the farm who often purchases the whole animal, breaking it down at the restaurant and making use of every element, from bones for stock to custom cuts for specials.

Overall, when John and Holly reflect on their work, they attribute their interactions with the community and engagement with fellow farmers and customers with bringing purpose to their roles as farmers. They've found joy in the intimate connection they've established with the ecosystem through daily chores like moving the mulch and the bedding to expose the natural transformation of the soil and observing the renewal of the pasture and grasslands, which grows back thicker after having been grazed by the farm's livestock.

John says the privilege of working with chefs has given them a far greater appreciation for the amount of work that's put into the food at their restaurants. The relationships they've built have underscored the kinship that exists between farmers, who nurture the soil to produce the raw materials, and chefs, who take those materials and transform them into edible masterpieces.

Smoked Pork Pozole Rojo

John Sheffy and Holly Petrillo, Adelante
with ingredients from Liberation Farmers and Meadowlark Organics

John Sheffy and Holly Petrillo of Liberation Farmers pay a visit to Oaxaca, Mexico, every January to pick coffee for their direct trade coffee roastery, Liberation Coffee. It's tradition for them to eat pozole at their favorite street stand, La Chefinita, on the evening they arrive. This recipe was inspired by those steaming bowls of pozole as well as the cooking they do with host farmers Elvira and Tomas, who taught them to make nixtamal, tortillas, tamales, and many other delicious foods. This connection inspired the Taco Tuesdays hosted at Adelante, which feature this fresh, warming dish.

This pozole is a simple hearty soup that brings out the flavor and texture of the locally grown, freshly nixtamalized Meadowlark Organics corn as well as the flavorful Liberation Farmers' pork hock, butchered and smoked by Niemuth's Chop Shop in Waupaca. Farm-grown chilies provide enough heat to warm the core and the fresh oregano adds an exciting herbal note.

Although this recipe is delicious as written, it is also easy to modify. Feel free to substitute your own combination of meat, broth, chilies, herbs, and vegetables for a unique take.

SERVES 8-10 AS A MAIN COURSE

For the corn:

2 pounds (1 quart) dry flint corn

2 tablespoon cal lime (also called pickling lime or calcium hydroxide)

2½ quarts water

For the broth:

1 large 2–3-pound smoked pork hock

1 gallon water

To nixtamalize the corn:

Rinse the corn and drain. Mix corn, cal, and water in a nonreactive pot. Bring to a boil and simmer gently for 5 minutes. Turn off the heat and leave the corn mixture covered overnight to nixtamalize.

The next day, gently mix the corn and cal solution with fresh water, massaging the corn to remove the outer layer of the seed. Drain and rinse again with fresh water. Set aside.

To prepare smoked pork hock and broth:

Place the smoked pork hock in a large pot that accommodates the meat, along with a full gallon of water. Bring the liquid to a simmer and cook for at least one hour or until meat is falling off the bone and the broth is flavorful and slightly heavier in body.

Strain the broth and allow meat and bones to cool enough to remove and discard the bones. Coarsely chop the meat and set aside.

ADELANTE

For the chili sauce:

8 dried chilies (ancho, guajillo, pasilla, or other dried ripe chili)

2 cups steaming hot water

2 tablespoons sunflower or other high-quality vegetable oil

1 small onion, diced

5–6 garlic cloves, diced

1 cup tomato sauce or 2–3 fresh tomatoes

1 teaspoon kosher salt

½ teaspoon cumin

3 teaspoons chopped fresh oregano or 1 teaspoon dried Mexican oregano

Optional garnish:

finely shredded cabbage, chopped fresh oregano, lime wedges

To prepare the chili sauce:

Carefully toast the chilies over a small flame or in a hot dry pan until the color of the skin turns bright red. Split and remove seeds, veins, and stems. Rinse chilies briefly and place them in a small pot. Pour steaming water over the chilies. Cover them and allow them to stand for 15 minutes to rehydrate.

While you are waiting for the chilies to rehydrate, heat the sunflower oil over medium heat and sauté the diced onions and garlic until slightly browned, taking care not to burn the garlic.

Place the rehydrated chilies along with their water into the jar of a blender along with the cooked onions and garlic, tomatoes, salt, cumin, and oregano. Puree until thoroughly liquified. If small pieces of chili remain, you can push the mixture through a fine strainer to refine the sauce, but this step is optional.

To finish the pozole:

Combine the broth, chopped meat, nixtamalized corn, and chili sauce in a soup pot. Simmer the soup gently for 1 hour or until the corn is tender but still a bit chewy. By this point, the corn will have increased in size and absorbed a lot of the broth (and flavor).

When you are ready to serve, garnish each bowl with finely shredded cabbage, a sprinkle of oregano, and a squeeze of fresh lime juice.

Deutsch Family Farm

Osseo, Wisconsin
deutschfamilyfarm.com

When Alison and Jim Deutsch established their farm in 2006, they chose to leave unfulfilling careers in favor of a life that put their love for food and their appreciation and respect for the land at the forefront. For the first few years, they worked for a woman whose husband had passed away, raising her livestock and assisting her in wrapping up her family's farm business. From there, they rented farmland until they'd established the funds to purchase 160 acres of their own in 2010.

They began by raising pigs, livestock they knew they could move easily from place to place. They also purposely chose older breeds (including Hampshire, Duroc, and Berkshire hogs) that hadn't been genetically modified for modern farming.

Once they'd purchased their own land (which came complete with wooded areas, plenty of room for pasturing animals, and fields where they could grow their own feed), they added Buckeye chickens and cows. Since there were already a few farms in the area raising livestock for beef, they opted for dairy cows instead. They also pursued organic certification for both their land and their dairy operations, but they committed to practices that went above and beyond the minimum requirements and

allowed them to produce tender, well-marbled pork, nutrient-dense eggs, and milk that's high in butterfat and complex flavor.

Prior to the COVID-19 pandemic, restaurants represented about half of the farm's business, with a variety of restaurants purchasing whole animals. So when the industry shut down, the Deutschs knew they needed to pivot. Instead of relying as much on restaurant sales, they began hosting pop-up markets and selling directly to consumers.

As restaurant sales have returned, they've regained business from about a half dozen restaurants, including The Informalist, which relies on the farm for its ham. Each restaurant's purchasing habits vary; some maintain standing orders, while others change things up from week to week. But since the Deutschs deliver directly to their restaurant customers, they're able to keep up with each eatery's requirements and accommodate the needs of the chefs. The family takes great pride in seeing the meat they've raised on the menus at local dining establishments.

Over time, Alison says, the farming landscape in their area has changed. Dairy and livestock farms have been disappearing in droves. It's a sobering phenomenon to watch, one that she says keeps them motivated to continue working hard. It also gives her hope that her teenage children will grow up with a desire to continue the legacy of farming that they've worked to build.

Ham and Peas

Chef Ella Wesenberg, The Informalist
with ham from Deutsch Family Farm

Chef Ella Wesenberg's English-inspired ham and peas was served as a spring small plate at The Informalist. But the smoky ham hock and fresh pea salad would be equally at home as a brunch plate accompanied by sunny-side up eggs and toast.

SERVES 4-6

For the ham hock:

2 smoked ham hocks (approximately 2 pounds)

8 cups chicken stock (preferably homemade)

For the pickled shallots:

1 cup water

½ cup champagne vinegar

1 teaspoon kosher salt

⅓ cup sugar

4 shallots, thinly sliced

For the pea salad:

2 cups cucumber, peeled, halved lengthwise, seeds removed, and sliced into ¼-inch half-moons

2 cups fresh sugar snap peas, blanched, sliced lengthwise on a bias

½ cup pickled shallots

3 tablespoons pickling liquid from the shallots

kosher salt and pepper, to taste

fresh mint and sorrel leaves for garnish

To prepare the ham:

Preheat oven to 300°F.

In an oven-safe braising pan, add the ham hocks and chicken stock. Cover with a lid and place in the oven. Cook for 2–3 hours, until the ham hock meat is tender and falls apart when pulled at with a fork.

Pull ham hock meat off the bone in medium-size pieces. Strain the remaining liquid with a fine sieve into a small pot. Place over medium-low heat, add the ham hock pieces, and reduce the liquid by half.

To prepare the shallots:

In a small saucepan, combine the water, vinegar, salt, and sugar and simmer over moderate heat until the sugar dissolves. Put the shallots in a small bowl or pint-size jar and pour the vinegar mixture on top. Refrigerate for at least 4 hours before using.

To plate:

Combine the ingredients for the pea salad in a medium bowl and toss gently.

Divide the salad between four and six plates, positioning it on one side of the plate and leaving any remaining pickling liquid behind in the bowl. Place the pulled ham hock on the opposite side of the plates, spooning the glazy ham stock on top. Garnish the salad with sorrel and mint.

THE INFORMALIST

Lambalot Acres

Augusta, Wisconsin

When Duane and Deanna Klindworth purchased their first ewes, they had a goal in mind: to assist in easing the shortage of domestically raised lamb. Despite growing demand, the United States imports over half of the lamb consumed across the country. So raising lambs simply made sense.

Both farmers earned their degrees in agriculture at the University of Wisconsin–River Falls prior to purchasing their first two-acre farm in Minnesota, along with a few ewes for breeding. Duane worked in the hog industry at the time, so raising lambs was a part-time venture. But it was a pursuit they were able to continue, even as his job required them to move to Missouri.

In 1999, they decided to move to Wisconsin. Deanna's family lived there, and they wanted their children to have the opportunity to get to know both sets of grandparents. At the time, the hog industry was going through a tough stretch, so Duane left his job and went to work on Deanna's brother's farm. But he hadn't yet given up on the notion of starting his own farm. So they continued to raise lambs on the side, selling meat at the local farmers market.

In 2004, they were able to purchase eighty acres of farmland from Deanna's grandparents, which they put to use by expanding their flock and planting fields of hay, corn, wheat, and soybeans. As their children grew older and started participating in 4H, the farm grew to include chickens, pigs, and steers. But sheep remained their mainstay.

The lambs at Lambalot Acres are grown using natural practices, without the use of hormones or antibiotics. The flock grazes on forty acres of land during the summer months, with trees and hills serving as natural windbreaks and a barn and pole shed offering shelter as the weather gets colder. Conventional crops are also grown on the farm using no-till planting methods, with cover crops used to support grazing and soil health.

Lambalot implements an accelerated lambing program, which allows them to maintain a consistent supply of lamb year-round, along with

chicken, pork, beef, and wool. The bulk of their income is derived from wholesale, farmers market, and retail sales. However, word of mouth in the local food scene has attracted some restaurant business for the farm, with eateries like Forage and The Informalist showcasing dishes using Lambalot Acres lamb on their menus.

Since lamb still tends to be viewed largely as a seasonal item in western Wisconsin, the locally procured lamb is often featured as a seasonal special. But the Klindworths work closely with restaurants that reach out to them, assisting them with identifying and procuring the cuts they need.

Duane says it's a pleasure to work with local restaurants and see the creativity they put into the dishes created with the farm's lamb. But, most of all, it's a pride point for their family to be able to provide high-quality, hormone-free meat that's so well regarded by chefs and members of the community.

Lamb Burger with Tzatziki Sauce and Tomato Chutney

Chef Joey Phillips, The Informalist
with lamb from Lambalot Acres

A delicious burger is great any time of the year, and these lamb burgers are no exception. But they scream summer when topped with refreshing Greek-inspired tzatziki sauce and slightly sweet tomato chutney (which stands in as a great alternative to ketchup). Even if you're a newcomer to lamb, you needn't worry that you won't like a lamb burger. The meat is flavorful and tender, particularly if you source your lamb from a reputable local producer like Lambalot Acres. Lamb burgers can be served medium or medium rare, just like a beef burger.

SERVES 4

For the chutney:

1 tablespoon extra virgin olive oil

2 teaspoons black mustard seeds

1 cup yellow onion, sliced

1½ tablespoons jalapeño, seeds removed and minced

1 tablespoon fresh ginger, peeled and minced

3 garlic cloves, sliced thinly

1 teaspoon ancho chili

1½ teaspoons cumin

1 teaspoon coriander

1 teaspoon chili

1 teaspoon turmeric

tiny pinch of allspice

1¼ pounds fresh tomatoes, blanched, peeled, and diced into medium pieces

1 tablespoon sugar

2 tablespoons sherry vinegar

kosher salt, to taste

For the tzatziki sauce:

1 cup plain whole milk yogurt

2 teaspoons fresh garlic, minced

1 cup cucumber, grated

pinch of dried sumac

2 tablespoons fresh lemon juice

¼ cup fresh dill, minced

½ teaspoon dried dill

1 cup fresh parsley, chiffonade

kosher salt, to taste

For the burger:

1½ pounds ground lamb, pattied into four 6-ounce portions

kosher salt

black pepper

4 brioche buns

butter

1 head of farm-fresh butterhead lettuce

tomato chutney

tzatziki sauce

THE INFORMALIST

To prepare the chutney:

In a small saucepan, heat the olive oil over medium heat and add the mustard seeds, stirring constantly until they start to pop. Add in the onions and sweat them until they turn translucent. Add in the jalapeño, ginger, and garlic, and cook for about 3 minutes. Add the rest of the spices and cook for another 3 minutes. Add the tomatoes and turn down to a low simmer to reduce for about 30 minutes until the tomatoes fall apart and the resulting sauce starts to thicken. Add the sugar and vinegar, and cook for a final 5 minutes. The result should be a shiny, glossy chutney. Season to taste with salt and allow to cool. The chutney can be made ahead of time and stored in an airtight container in the refrigerator. The chutney will keep well for 4–6 weeks in the refrigerator.

To prepare the tzatziki sauce:

Mix all the ingredients in a bowl. Season to taste with salt. The tzatziki can be made a day ahead and stored in an airtight container in the refrigerator. Liquid may separate from the sauce overnight; just stir it back into the sauce.

To prepare the burger:

Preheat grill. Season your lamb patties with salt and pepper and grill over medium-high heat to desired temperature (145° for medium rare). Lightly butter each side of the brioche buns and toast them on the grill until browned. While you make the burgers, warm the tomato chutney in a small saucepan over low heat.

To assemble:

Place a leaf or two of butterhead lettuce on the bottom of the bun; add the lamb patty, the warm tomato chutney, the tzatziki sauce, and finally the top of the bun.

Lakeview Buffalo Farm

Belgium, Wisconsin
lakeviewbuffalofarm.com

Al Weyker didn't start out as a bison (American buffalo) farmer. He began his career as a fifth-generation dairy farmer on his family's 230-acre farm along the beautiful shores of Lake Michigan. He was just sixteen years old when he took over operations of his parents' farm alongside his brother. He worked for his parents until he got married, transitioning to running his own farm on their land in 1973 and purchasing the property in 1981.

For years, he ran the farm as a dairy operation with his wife, Barbara, and their six children. But in 1996, he decided to try something different. Intrigued by the low maintenance needed to raise bison, a species not only native to Wisconsin but also one that produces lean meat with a high nutritional value, he purchased six young bulls from another Wisconsin farmer.

In the beginning, they started by marketing the meat to friends and family, but as demand grew, Al saw that he would need to increase the size of his herd. So, in 2001, he sold off his dairy herd and began

PAUL WEYKER

purchasing bison calves to raise on pasture. When a heifer inadvertently sneaked into their herd of bulls, they began breeding their own stock.

To reduce the stress for the herd, calves are raised alongside their mothers until a new batch of calves is born. At that point, they are moved to a new pasture where their feed is monitored with the goal of raising consistently sized bulls.

Over the years, the farm has sold to numerous grocers, including Saukville Meats and Quality Cut Meats in Cascade, Wisconsin, while Al's grandchildren continue to sell the farm's bison at the Milwaukee Winter Farmers Market each year. But Al has also cultivated relationships with chefs from smaller restaurants, including Five O'Clock Club and Braise in Milwaukee, which have the flexibility to operate with smaller quantities of meat or variable cuts for specials.

For years before retiring to care for her parents in California, Chef Jan Kelley used Lakeview bison shanks for osso bucco at restaurants including Barossa and Meritage. Joe Muench of Black Shoe Hospitality has been a regular customer for years, purchasing a wide variety of cuts (including short ribs, shanks, and off-cuts) for use at restaurants such as Story Hill BKC and, more recently, Buttermint Finer Dining & Cocktails.

Meanwhile, stalwart customers have included Libby Montana's in Mequon, which purchases meat for burgers, and Chef Andy Tenaglia of Lagniappe Brasserie in New Berlin, who has also staffed the booth for the Wisconsin Bison Producers stall at the Wisconsin State Fair, ensuring that the meats from Lakeview Buffalo farm and another local Wisconsin brand are well represented.

At its peak, Lakeview Buffalo farm raised up to 140 bison at a time, but eventually they pared down the herd. Today, Al raises about 50 bulls on his land and—while he hopes to continue raising animals for a few more years—his daughter, Jennifer, and her children, Sam and Alexandra, are in line to take over the family farm when he decides it's time to step away.

Buffalo Liver with Maple Bacon, Chard, Rosti, and Cherry Port Wine Sauce

Chef Joe Muench, Buttermint Finer Dining & Cocktails
with American buffalo from Lakeview Buffalo Farm

Since Chef Joe Muench was a child, he's harbored an affection for any type of liver, from braunschweiger and liver sausage to duck liver, which he loves since it can be prepared medium rare. In the summer, his family would pack up their station wagon and head out on vacation, often stopping at Howard Johnson's restaurants as they traveled. As early as the age of five, he would shock the restaurants' servers by ordering liver and onions. They would often turn to his mother and ask, "Is this for real?" To this day, whenever he prepares chicken for the grill, the liver becomes a coveted "chef's snack." As for this dish, he says it might well be a contender for his last meal, paired with a good pinot noir or IPA.

SERVES 3-4

For the maple bacon:

½ pound Usinger's bacon

2–3 tablespoons Little Man Maple Syrup

1 teaspoon black pepper

For the braised chard:

2 tablespoons butter

1 medium onion, diced

16 ounces Swiss chard leaves and stems, thoroughly washed and chopped

1 bay leaf

2 cups chicken or vegetable broth

kosher salt and black pepper, to taste

For the port wine sauce:

1 tablespoon butter

1 shallot, chopped

1 fresh rosemary sprig

1 teaspoon whole black peppercorns

2 bay leaves

1 cup port wine

1 cup frozen tart cherries, finely chopped (reserve 3 tablespoons)

¼ cup brandy

1 cup chicken demi-glace

1 cup veal demi-glace

kosher salt, to taste

For the rosti:

2 pounds Yukon Gold potatoes

¼ cup roasted garlic, must be very soft and mashed

6 tablespoons clarified butter, divided

¾ teaspoon kosher salt

½ teaspoon black pepper

pinch of coarse salt

For the buffalo liver:

6 four-ounce slices of American buffalo liver

kosher salt

black pepper

2 tablespoons clarified butter

½ cup all-purpose flour

2 tablespoons whole butter

For the garnish:

fresh chives, minced

fresh sage leaves

black pepper

To prepare the maple bacon:

Preheat the oven to 350°F.

Place the bacon strips on a parchment-lined baking sheet with some space between each slice.

Brush each strip with the maple syrup, brushing several times to help build layers of syrup. Sprinkle the bacon evenly with the pepper. Bake for 15–20 minutes until the bacon is browned and crispy. Remove from the oven and transfer the bacon to a clean sheet pan or plate. Set aside.

To prepare the braised chard:

Place butter and onions in a heavy pot or Dutch oven and sweat over medium heat until the onions have turned translucent. Do not allow the onions to brown. Add the chard and sweat for 4–5 minutes. Add the bay leaf and broth to the pot. Cover and simmer for 15–20 minutes. Taste the liquor (broth) and then season with salt and pepper to taste. Continue to simmer for another 5–10 minutes or until tender. Set aside and keep warm.

To prepare the port wine sauce:

In a heavy-bottomed saucepan, melt the butter over medium heat and add the shallots. Sweat the shallots for 3–4 minutes, and then add the rosemary, peppercorns, and bay leaves. Sweat the shallots and aromatics for 3–4 minutes. Add the port wine and all but the 3 tablespoons of reserved chopped cherries and reduce the liquid by half. Add in the brandy and reduce by half. Finally, add the chicken and veal demi-glace and simmer until the sauce is thick enough to coat the back of a metal spoon. While the sauce is simmering, skim any impurities that come to the top. Strain the sauce into a heat-proof container, through a wire mesh strainer, pressing the sauce to get as much as possible into the container. Taste for salt, and then add the reserved 3 tablespoons of cherries and keep warm.

To prepare the rosti:

Peel and grate the potatoes using a box grater, making as many long strands as possible. Grab handfuls of potato and squeeze out excess liquid, and then place in a mixing bowl. Add roasted garlic, 2 tablespoons clarified butter, salt and pepper, and toss to thoroughly combine.

Melt 2 tablespoons of clarified butter in a 10-inch cast-iron or nonstick pan over medium-low heat. Place the potato mixture in the pan, but do not pack it down. Use a rubber spatula to bring the edges together, and then lightly pat down to even the surface. Cook for 12 minutes on the first side or until the underside is very golden and crispy, lifting the edge with a spatula to check. Add more butter if the pan seems dry. If the potatoes are not turning golden after 5–6 minutes, increase the heat.

To flip, cover the pan with a pan lid or round pizza pan. Flip the rosti out onto the cover quickly and with confidence, and then slide it back into the cooking pan to cook the other side. To cook the second side, add more butter and cook for 8–12 minutes until golden and crispy.

Slide the finished rosti onto a cutting board, and season with a pinch of coarse salt; cut into four or six wedges and serve immediately. To keep warm if not serving immediately, transfer to a rack-lined sheet tray and place in a 225°F oven until ready to serve.

To prepare the buffalo liver:

Place the liver on a sheet pan and pat each side dry with paper towels. Evenly season each side with salt and pepper. Heat a frying pan over medium heat until hot but not sizzling. Add the clarified butter to the pan to melt. Lightly dredge the liver slices in the flour shaking off the excess.

Make sure not to overcrowd the pan by cooking the liver two to three slices at a time. Place the slices one by one in the pan, shaking the pan slightly and lightly browning on the first side for 3–4 minutes. Flip the slices and add a tablespoon of the whole butter. Cook for 3–4 minutes on the second side before transferring to a baking sheet to keep warm until serving. Medium rare is the desired doneness.

To plate:

Using a slotted spoon to remove the chard from its liquor, arrange it on individual plates or a large platter to create a base. Be sure to reserve the liquor; it's wonderful for dunking warm buttered bread. Randomly arrange the rosti on the plate or platter, taking care not to let it sit directly on the chard. Lay a slice of liver onto each wedge of rosti so it's half-way covering the rosti wedges. Top some of the liver slices with the port wine sauce and drizzle more around the plates or the platter. Serve any extra sauce on the side. Lay slices of the bacon next to or on top of the liver. Finish the dish with the chives, sage, and freshly ground black pepper.

Wisconsin Grass-Fed Beef Cooperative

Viroqua, Wisconsin
wisconsinmeadows.com

Collective values bring farmers together. The desire to improve their farming practices breeds shared knowledge and education. And working together ensures longevity, fair pricing, and the production of the highest-quality food possible.

Such is the case for the Wisconsin Grass-Fed Beef Cooperative, a group of more than 230 farmers who use sustainable practices to raise 100 percent grass-fed beef and pastured pork products in Wisconsin.

The cooperative was founded in 2008 by a group of livestock producers who saw the advantage in coming together to market their high-quality meats to a larger market. They were all concerned about animal welfare, and many had begun experimenting with intentional and rotational grazing practices. They all loved their jobs raising cattle, but they didn't love the work of marketing their products and fighting for premium prices.

A cooperative model allowed them to work together to develop a tiered system that ensures consistency between products, and since raising 100 percent grass-fed cattle takes a longer period of time, the cooperative also

ensures that the farms receive a premium price for their product. Perhaps most important, it offered farmers a mechanism for marketing their local products under a consistent, recognizable brand: Wisconsin Meadows.

To ensure consistency, every farm who is a member-owner of the cooperative signs an affidavit, attesting to the protocols they follow on their farms, and all agree to operate using regenerative sustainability practices that prohibit the use of genetically modified organisms (GMOs) and chemicals. That includes raising their animals without the use of steroids or corn-based feed.

Oversight for the cooperative is provided by a board of directors, who direct a management team that deals directly with the farms and oversees the safety, processing, distribution, and traceability of their products, which are delivered to restaurants and grocery stores throughout the upper Midwest.

Restaurants can take advantage of traditional distribution channels, but they can also work directly with the cooperative to place special orders, including ordering prime cuts they can butcher themselves. Consumers will find the cooperative's high-quality meats displayed on plates at restaurants across the state, including Braise, La Merenda, and Morel.

In addition to working on behalf of the farmers, the cooperative promotes consumer education through initiatives like pasture walks during the summer months, during which both farmers and consumers can tour farms and better understand how they operate.

Braised Short Ribs with Moong Dal Curry

Dave Swanson, Braise
with short ribs from the Wisconsin Grass-Fed Beef Cooperative

Succulent, slow-cooked beef short ribs are a classic dish that should be in everyone's repertoire. But Chef Dave Swanson gives the classic dish a global upgrade by pairing it with a fragrant quick-cooking Indian curry that stands in for the usual mashed potatoes.

Note: While the short ribs and dal are fantastic served together, each of these recipes can stand on its own. For a classic winter dinner, serve the short ribs over creamy polenta or spaetzle with fresh, seasonal vegetables. Or pair the quick-cooking dal with rice or flatbread for a quick vegetarian meal.

SERVES 6

For the braised short ribs:

5 pounds short ribs

kosher salt and pepper, to taste

3 tablespoons vegetable oil

2 yellow onions, sliced

6 garlic cloves, minced

1 quart beef stock

2 tablespoons dark brown sugar

2 tablespoon red wine vinegar or cider vinegar

4 sprigs of parsley

4 sprigs of thyme

2 bay leaves

moong dal curry (recipe follows)

Optional garnish:

minced fresh cilantro or parsley

To prepare the braised short ribs:

Dry short ribs with paper towels, and season with salt and pepper. Heat 2 tablespoons of oil over medium-high heat in a Dutch oven. When the oil is beginning to smoke, add half of the beef. Cook on the first side, without moving, until browned (about 2–3 minutes). Turn short ribs over and brown on the other side. Transfer to a dish. If the browned bits on the bottom of the pan are getting too dark, add some stock, scrape up the brown bits, and then pour the liquid into the bowl with the short ribs. Add more oil, and brown the remaining short ribs.

Reduce the heat to medium and add oil (if needed). Add onions, cooking until they are lightly browned, followed by garlic. Add the stock, brown sugar, and vinegar. Scrape up any additional browned bits, and then add the short ribs and aromatics.

Increase the heat and bring to a simmer. Simmer over very low heat for about 2–3 hours or until the short ribs are tender.

To plate:

Scoop a generous portion of moong dal into a large shallow bowl. Arrange short ribs over the top, spooning a bit of jus over the top. Sprinkle with minced cilantro or parsley and serve.

Moong Dal Curry

SERVES 4 AS A VEGETARIAN MAIN DISH

For the curry:

1 cup yellow moong dal (split yellow mung beans)

2 cups water

1 teaspoon curry powder

1 tablespoon vegetable oil

For the tadka:

3 tablespoons vegetable oil

1 teaspoon cumin seeds

2 teaspoons yellow mustard seeds

2 teaspoons brown mustard seeds

1 small red onion, peeled and minced

1 teaspoon grated ginger

1 or 2 whole dried red chilies, crushed

2 garlic cloves

1 small tomato, finely chopped (optional)

1 cup coconut milk

salt, to taste

1 tablespoon minced fresh cilantro

To prepare the curry:

Pick through the dal and remove any debris. Rinse the dal well under running water in a fine-mesh sieve. Drain thoroughly.

In a deep saucepan, bring water, curry powder, and vegetable oil to a boil over high heat. Add dal. Reduce heat to medium-low and cook (uncovered) for 30 minutes, stirring occasionally, until dal is very soft. If the water starts to dry up, add another ½ cup water. Remove from heat and set aside.

To prepare the tadka:

In a medium skillet, heat 3 tablespoons of oil over medium-high heat. Add cumin seeds and mustard seeds; when they begin to sizzle, add onion. Sauté for 7–8 minutes, until onion is well browned. Add ginger, chilies, and garlic (and tomato if using). Cook, stirring occasionally, for another 8 minutes; add moong dal mixture, coconut milk, and salt. Bring to a simmer and check seasoning. Keep warm, adding cilantro just before serving.

The moong dal curry can be made ahead and gently reheated before serving with the short ribs.

Klatt Farms

Barron, Wisconsin
facebook.com/KlattFarmsWI

As the sun rises across the fields at Klatt Farms, you might glimpse a barn cat slinking along the fence line, a goat frolicking in the field, or a horse grazing in the pasture alongside a herd of cattle. But you're also likely to see a father and son chopping hay for silage, a grandfather toting his grandchildren through the fields on a Gator, or a mother introducing her newborn to the sights and smells of the farm.

This multigenerational farm began as a dairy operation when Michael and Jane Klatt purchased a 120-acre farm in 1988. For twenty years, they milked a herd of dairy cattle before selling their cows in 2008. From there, their son Sean took over the farm on a land contract, continuing the dairy operation for nine more years before converting the farm to beef production in 2017.

Today Sean operates the livestock farm alongside his wife, Danielle; his son, Mason; and their daughter, Madisyn, with help and encouragement from countless family members, all of whom put the word family into the notion of a family farm.

Klatt Farms operates with approximately one hundred heads of Angus cross cattle, which are raised from calfhood and fed a forage-based diet of farm-grown corn and alfalfa haylage custom mixed with soybean meal. Unlike corn-finished cattle, they are fed a consistent diet over the course of their life spans. The cows' diet is developed with the assistance of a nutritionist and consultations with their butcher to keep tabs on the flavor and fat content, ensuring consistency in their USDA-inspected beef. The cattle are raised on a staggered schedule, allowing the Klatts to butcher six steers per month all year long.

Most beef is sold to local consumers via direct marketing with pickup and deliveries of guaranteed-weight packages available on a monthly basis. In 2021, they piloted a beef community-supported agriculture program in the Eau Claire market, during which customers purchased one-eighth of a steer over an eight-week period. Marketing for the farm's offerings is done primarily through Facebook, where the farm shares family stories and information about daily farm life while educating consumers about their farming practices.

But the Klatts also work with a few local restaurants, most notably The Lakely at the Oxbow Hotel in Eau Claire. Each month, the farm works closely with Chef Luke Bilda to custom-butcher a full steer each month, using a nose-to-tail approach that makes use of every part of the cattle from soup bones to various cuts including prime rib, roasts, and ground beef.

The family also worked with The Lakely to host a beef-focused dinner during which they were able to talk with consumers about their nontraditional approach to raising cattle.

Working with restaurants is a pride point for the Klatts, who have worked hard to design a business plan and farming model that produces safe, nutritious, and superior-tasting beef—a model they feel good about passing on to the next passionate generation of family farmers.

Chef Bilda's Braised Red Wine Beef

Chef Luke Bilda, The Lakely with beef from Klatt Farms

With a technique passed along to him by an early mentor, Chef Luke Bilda has carried this recipe with him for twenty years. He says the main ingredient in the dish is love, and he encourages liberal use of it. He endorses the local Klatt Farms beef he uses at the restaurant as some of the best he's ever had in the area.

THE LAKELY

SERVES 4-6

For the horseradish gremolata:

zest from 1 lemon

1 bunch parsley, finely chopped

2 cloves garlic, grated or minced

1 cup prepared horseradish, squeezed dry

For the beef:

5-6 pounds chuck roast

1 cup flour

2 tablespoons cooking oil

4 celery ribs, roughly chopped

1 onion, roughly chopped

2 large carrots, roughly chopped

2 garlic cloves

¼ cup tomato paste

1 cup dry red wine (Cabernet or Merlot)

6 cups beef stock or broth

1 sprig rosemary

1 sprig thyme

To prepare the gremolata:

Combine all ingredients in a small bowl. Set aside.

To prepare the beef:

Preheat the oven to 325°F.

Dust the chuck roast completely with the flour. Heat braising pan or Dutch oven with cooking oil on medium-high heat. Brown roast on all sides, turning down the heat as needed to prevent scorching. Remove roast from pan.

Add celery, onion, carrot, and garlic to the pan. Cook vegetables until onions are translucent, while scraping the pan drippings off the bottom of the pan. Clear a space on the bottom of the pan and add tomato paste and mix with vegetables. Deglaze the pan with the red wine, bring to a boil and reduce the wine by half.

Add beef, stock, rosemary, and thyme, and bring to a simmer. Cover and place in the oven for 4-5 hours until fork-tender.

Remove from the oven and remove beef from the pan. Strain liquid from the solids, reserving the braising liquid. Over medium heat, simmer the braising liquid in pan until the sauce coats a spoon. When sauce has thickened, return beef to the pan to coat with sauce before serving.

To serve, sprinkle gremolata on top of beef and plate with potatoes and vegetables of your choosing.

Braised Beef Short Ribs with Dill Spaetzle and Sour Cherry Jus

Chef de Cuisine Mike Meinzer, Third Coast Provisions with vegetables from Centgraf Farms

Over the years, Third Coast Provisions and its sister restaurant, Flourchild Pizza, have cultivated a great relationship with Nicole Centgraf and her family at Centgraf Farms. As a result, both restaurants source a high percentage of their seasonal ingredients from the farm, using much of it fresh but also preserving large quantities for the winter months.

This short rib dish takes advantage of that farm-fresh produce in a variety of ways. Chef Mike Meinzer features green beans, carrots, and mushrooms as an accompaniment for the short ribs. But you can feel free to use any seasonal vegetables you have on hand.

While this recipe has multiple components, many can be made ahead of time. Don't hesitate to get a head start on some of the elements (including the dill spaetzle and tomato water) to save yourself some time.

SERVES 4

For the dill spaetzle:

2 eggs

½ cup fresh dill, chopped

1 cup sour cream

2 teaspoons kosher salt

1¾–2 cups all-purpose flour

2–3 tablespoons sunflower oil
(for searing)

For the tomato water:

2½ pounds tomatoes, cut into quarters
(this is a great use for blemished
tomatoes)

10 garlic cloves

1 tablespoon kosher salt

2 tablespoons white sugar

2 tablespoons whole black peppercorns

½ ounce fresh thyme

2 bay leaves

For the beef:

4 boneless beef short ribs (8–9 ounces
each)

4 tablespoons kosher salt

2 tablespoons black pepper

½ cup sunflower oil

2 carrots, diced

1 white onion, diced

½ stalk celery, diced

8 garlic cloves, smashed

2 cups red wine

4 cups chicken stock

2 tablespoons whole black peppercorns

1 ounce fresh thyme

4 bay leaves (fresh, if possible)

For the sour cherry jus:

4 ounces unsalted butter

½ cup shallots, thinly sliced

2 garlic cloves, minced

½ cup red wine

½ cup white sugar

½ cup water

1½ cups sherry vinegar

2 tablespoons Dijon mustard

4 cups sour cherries (frozen or fresh)

2 cups braising liquid from short ribs

1 tablespoon kosher salt

2 teaspoons black pepper

1 tablespoon dried mustard seeds

For the vegetables:

5 tablespoons unsalted butter, divided

¼ cup shallots, thinly sliced

12 ounces green beans, blanched

8 ounces heirloom carrots, blanched

2 cups fresh mushrooms, chopped

2 cups tomato water

4 cups seared spaetzle

½ cup chopped herbs (chives, parsley, tarragon)

To finish the beef:

2 tablespoons unsalted butter

2 tablespoons chopped fresh herbs

To prepare the spaetzle:

In a stand mixer, combine the eggs, dill, sour cream, and salt. Mix on low for about a minute, and then add 1¾ cups flour. Continue to mix for about 3 minutes on low until the dough comes together. The dough should be on the thicker side. If dough is too sticky, mix in an additional ¼ cup flour. Set dough aside and let rest for 10 minutes.

On the stove, bring a pot of water to a simmer over medium heat. Spray a perforated hotel pan (or any spaetzle maker or colander) with a little oil; it will help the dough feed through the pan. Place your pan or colander over the pot of water. Working In small batches, push the spaetzle dough through the pan with a spatula, forming small dumplings. Let the spaetzle cook in water for 3 minutes until they float, and then remove with a slotted spoon and put into a colander to drain excess water. Once all the spaetzle is cooked, pat dry (or let sit in the fridge to dry out overnight).

Once the spaetzle is dry, coat the bottom of a large sauté pan with sunflower oil over high heat. When oil is hot, carefully drop in handfuls of spaetzle until the bottom of the pan is covered. Turn heat down to medium-high and let spaetzle sear for about 3 minutes or until it becomes golden. Toss the spaetzle in the pan or stir with a rubber spatula or spoon to get a nice golden color on all sides of the spaetzle. Once a golden brown crust has formed, remove spaetzle and pat dry. Repeat with remaining spaetzle in batches.

To prepare the tomato water:

In a large metal bowl that can sit on top of a saucepan, combine all ingredients. Cover the bowl with two layers of plastic wrap. Then take a larger piece of plastic wrap and tie it tightly around the rim of the bowl to secure the two layers. Place the saucepan on the stove and fill halfway with water. Bring the water to a boil and place the metal bowl filled with the tomato mixture on top, making sure the water does not touch the bottom of the bowl. Let the tomatoes cook for an hour, checking the pot periodically to make sure there is still water in the bottom. Bring water to boil in a tea kettle and add more hot water to

the saucepan as needed. After the tomatoes have been steaming for an hour, carefully remove plastic wrap and pour the tomatoes into a strainer lined with cheese-cloth and placed over a bowl. Press the tomatoes to encourage them to release all of their liquid. Once all liquid has drained out, set the fragrant tomato water aside. Discard the tomato solids.

To prepare the beef:

Preheat the oven to 300°F.

Season short ribs with salt and pepper. Heat sunflower oil in a large pan over medium-high heat. Add the short ribs to the pan and sear until a nice crust has formed on each side, turning as needed. This process should take about 6–8 minutes. Remove the ribs from the pan.

Add in carrots, white onion, celery, garlic, and caramel-ize for about 8 minutes; then deglaze with red wine. Add chicken stock, whole black peppercorns, fresh thyme, and bay leaves. Cover with foil, and place the pan into the oven and cook for 2 hours. Remove from the oven and set aside 2 cups of the braising liquid to use for the cherry jus.

To prepare the sour cherry jus:

Melt butter in a large saucepan over medium heat. Add the shallots and garlic, and cook for 4–5 minutes or until they begin to soften. Add the red wine and reduce. Then add the remaining ingredients and bring to a boil. Allow the mixture to boil and reduce for about 8–10 minutes or until the sauce has thickened (the thicker, the better). Once the sauce is thickened, set aside.

To prepare the vegetables:

Melt 3 tablespoons of butter over medium-high heat in a sauté pan. Add shallots, blanched vegetables, and mushrooms. Sauté for 3–4 minutes. Add the tomato water and reduce until the sauce thickens. Add cooked spaetzle, 2 tablespoons of butter, and chopped herbs and toss until evenly coated. Season with salt to taste.

To finish the beef and plate the dish:

Place the short ribs in a small pan over medium heat. As the short ribs reheat, pour some of the cherry jus over the top. Add 2 tablespoons butter and 2 tablespoons chopped herbs. Turn and coat the ribs in the sauce.

To serve:

Place a portion of the spaetzle-vegetable mix in the bottom of a shallow bowl, top with a braised short rib, and spoon cherry jus over the top.

Stone Bank Farm

Oconomowoc, Wisconsin
stonebankmarket.com

When you look out across Stone Bank Farm's seventy-five acres of land, you'll see mostly pasture. There are Red Devon cattle, sheep, and pigs. There's a smaller three-acre plot that accommodates greenhouses and vegetable gardens. And right in the center of the land, there's a historic church that has been converted into a public marketplace, where vegetables and prepared food products are sold to the public year-round.

At Stone Bank, they grow their own feed for the lambs, and pigs pasture in the surrounding woods. Beehives contribute to the pollination of vegetables while producing honey that is sold at the market. Along with farm produce, Wisconsin cheeses, and shelf-stable items such as Wisconsin-grown and -milled grains, jams made with locally procured fruit, granola, and beans, Stone Bank offers prepared foods and made-to-order lunches. It's a place where consumers can experience the bounty of locally grown and pastured food products.

STONE BANK FARM

The land has been farmed since the 1850s. But the farm that exists today was built on a vision. When John Gehl purchased the acreage in 2003 on behalf of the Faye Gehl Conservation Foundation, he did so with the intention of preserving the land and preventing it from being developed. But that vision has grown to include efforts to educate the community about locally grown, nutrient-dense food. And it has done so while employing talented people who share a passion for regenerative farming practices that not only produce healthful food but also maintain a respect for the soil.

Today, the Stone Bank Farm vision continues to evolve, influenced both by those who cultivate the soil and raise the animals and by passionate evangelists like Michele Relford, a family friend who manages the property and invests her time in forging connections between the community, the farm, and the food it produces. It's being shaped by local consumers who choose to support the farm's mission by purchasing produce and foods prepared in the Stone Bank commercial kitchen. Increasingly, it's also being shaped by chefs like Kyle Knall of Birch, who has not only invested in the farm by purchasing its goods—including its grass-fed beef—but also contributed his talents to creating the prepared food menu at the market and cooking for the farm's greenhouse dinners, which celebrate the bounty that the land has produced.

Grass-Fed Beef with Charred Summer Squash, Salsa Verde, and Country Ham Crumble

Chef Kyle Knall, Birch
with grass-fed beef from Stone Bank Farm

Chef Kyle Knall is a fan of the complex flavor of Stone Bank Farm's grass-fed beef. However, using the right cooking technique is key to unlocking the flavor and tenderness in grass-fed meat. When cooking grass-fed meat, it is important to prepare the meat properly: season it ahead of time, build a crust by cooking it over high heat, baste with herbs and butter, and let it rest the appropriate amount of time. Chef Knall notes that butter is a key component since the milk solids caramelize on the meat and build a nice crust.

This recipe pairs beautifully cooked steak with bright fresh flavors in a dish that makes the most of mid- to late summer.

SERVES 4

For country ham crumble:

1 tablespoon canola oil

½ cup chopped country ham

½ cup old toasted bread

For salsa verde:

½ cup canola oil

2 garlic cloves

2 tablespoon sea salt

2 bunches cilantro

½ cup olive oil

To prepare the country ham crumble:

Heat 1 tablespoon of oil in a 10-inch cast-iron skillet or heavy-bottomed skillet over medium heat. Add chopped country ham and fry for 8 minutes, stirring occasionally, until the ham renders and becomes crispy.

To make the crumble, blitz the fried ham and toasted bread in a food processor until they resemble wet sand. Set aside.

To prepare the salsa verde:

Place the canola oil, garlic, and sea salt in a blender and blend thoroughly. Add the herbs and olive oil and blitz for an additional 15 seconds. Pour into a bowl and set aside.

For summer squash:

2 whole summer squash (zucchini is preferable)

4 tablespoons olive oil, divided

kosher salt

cracked black pepper

3 tablespoons fresh lime juice

For marinated tomatoes:

1 cup halved cherry tomatoes

1½ tablespoons olive oil

1 tablespoon red wine vinegar

kosher salt

freshly cracked black pepper

6–8 fresh basil leaves

For the steak:

4 6–8-ounce portions of grass-fed flat iron, New York strip, or ribeye steak

kosher salt

freshly cracked black pepper

1 bunch thyme

1 bunch rosemary

8 tablespoons unsalted butter, melted

To prepare summer squash:

Cut the squash in half lengthwise and season with 2 tablespoons olive oil, kosher salt, and cracked pepper. Grill or sear the squash in a pan until golden brown on the cut side, cooking it 80 percent of the way. Then flip it and cook for another minute. It is important not to over-cook. As soon as you remove the squash from the grill, put it on a plate and season it with the remaining olive oil and all the lime juice. Allow squash to sit and marinate while you finish preparing the steak.

To prepare the marinated tomatoes:

In a small bowl, mix the halved cherry tomatoes with the olive oil and vinegar. Season with salt and freshly cracked pepper to taste. Set aside. Chop basil and toss with tomatoes just before serving.

To prepare the steak:

Season the steak with kosher salt and freshly cracked black pepper and allow it to sit at room temperature for 5 minutes before cooking. While it sits, create your herb brush by bundling the thyme and rosemary together and tying them with kitchen twine.

Pat the meat dry with a paper towel to remove any mois-ture that the salt has pulled out of the meat. Place meat on a hot grill. Flip the meat within 20 seconds so that the meat scruffs up and creates more surface area to car-amelize. As soon as the meat is flipped, baste the hot side with the herb brush dipped in melted butter. Con-tinue this process until the grass-fed meat is cooked to medium rare (130°). When the steaks hit temperature, pull them off the grill and let the meat rest on a rack for half the amount of time it took to cook. This step is extremely important so that the juices redistribute throughout the beef.

To serve:

Spread salsa verde in the middle of a large platter or on individual plates. Slice beef and arrange on top of the salsa. Place one squash half cut-side up next to the beef, and top with country ham crumble. Place marinated cherry tomatoes and fresh basil leaves around the plate to finish.

Sweet Treats

Recipes

Featured Farms

Sweet Cream Frozen Custard

Chef Kurt Fogle, Dairyland Old-Fashioned
Frozen Custard & Hamburgers
with dairy from Sassy Cow Creamery

While a home ice cream machine will never produce custard with the same rich, silky texture as commercial equipment, the use of fresh, high-quality dairy will make a significant difference in its flavor. This custard shines when served with farm-fresh berries or a drizzle of maple syrup.

Note: You want to get custard mix where it's going quickly. Cook it quickly, cool it quickly, and spin it quickly.

MAKES 1 QUART

3¼ cups whole milk

1¼ cups heavy cream

3 tablespoons skim milk powder

1 cup granulated sugar

1 teaspoon sea salt

4 egg yolks

¼ cup honey

Before you begin, sanitize your workspace, your hands, and your utensils.

Pour the milk and cream into a saucepan and add the milk powder, sugar, and salt. Whisk in the egg yolks and honey.

Heat the mixture, stirring constantly, until it registers 185° on a candy thermometer. Remove the custard from the heat and strain it into a bowl over an ice bath to cool it down quickly. Stir to chill and store overnight in the refrigerator to mature.

When ready to churn, use a hand blender or conventional blender—or at least a whisk—to mix the custard again before you pour it into the ice cream maker. Churn according to the manufacturer's instructions. Transfer the finished ice cream to an airtight container and place in the freezer until ready to serve.

Dairyland Old-Fashioned Frozen Custard & Hamburgers

Frozen custard is ubiquitous in Wisconsin. But custard made on site with 100 percent Wisconsin dairy is a rarity, even in the Dairy State. It's just one of the elements that sets Dairyland Old-Fashioned Frozen Custard & Hamburgers apart.

When Dairyland launched their brand in 2020, they did so with a commitment to steward and showcase elements of Wisconsin's rich food culture. Among their goals was building a model for operations that directly supported Wisconsin farmers while showcasing the exceptional quality and flavor of Wisconsin dairy products.

So when Dr. Scott Rankin (aka Dr. Ice Cream), associate professor in food science at the University of Wisconsin–Madison, strongly suggested they consider making a frozen custard that highlighted the nuanced flavors of locally sourced cream, the Dairyland team made it their mission to create an alternative to vanilla custard that highlights the rich flavors inherent to high-quality milk.

Head to Dairyland and you'll find some of the most richly flavored, beautifully textured custard in the state in over 350 rotating flavors, including vanilla and chocolate. But it's their sweet cream custard that best showcases the quality of the milk they source from Sassy Cow Creamery in Columbus, Wisconsin.

Three Brothers Farm

Oconomowoc, Wisconsin
3brothersfarmwi.com

It was 1954 when Francis and Jacqui Gutschenritter purchased the hundred-acre farm in Oconomowoc that would eventually become Three Brothers Farm. Francis loved farming, but he wasn't sure he could make a living with the farm alone, so for years he rented out a portion of the land to others. But when he passed away and the farm was set to be put up for sale, his grandson Michael, who was living in Colorado at the time, decided to move home and take on a new career.

In 2013, Michael Gutschenritter began the work of converting the acreage from broad acre corn and soy into a place where he could grow food. Ultimately, he established Three Brothers Farm with about a dozen chickens and a community-supported agriculture (CSA) program. By 2016, he was joined by his wife, Courtney, whom he'd met at the University of Wisconsin–Stevens Point. She'd pursued work on a farm as part of an AmeriCorps program and loved it so much that she continued to pursue agricultural work, traveling across the globe before returning to Wisconsin, where she started a business growing flowers. The two reconnected at an agricultural conference and fell in love.

Together, they purchased Michael's family's land and began operating the farm together. The following year, they decided to drop the CSA in favor of focusing on pasturing animals, largely converting the farm to produce eggs.

Today, they maintain a flock of twenty-five hundred laying hens that are moved daily onto fresh pasture during the growing season and wintered in a large greenhouse with plenty of straw, leaves, and woodchips to peck through. The farm is home to sixty Shetland sheep raised for their meat and soft warm wool, which is used for both woven blankets and sheepskins. They also custom-graze twenty-four heifers for Koepke Dairy, which uses the milk to make their Wisconsin Original Labelle cheese.

Over the years, as Michael became an expert in his field, he created a unique grazing system called the HenPen, plans for which are sold through the Three Brothers Farm website. The system allows farmers to move their Electronet fencing, along with chicken coops, for ease or rotational grazing for laying hens and turkeys.

As the farm began to establish itself, restaurants began to inquire about purchasing eggs. In 2014, when Chef Peter Sandroni of La Merenda opened his second restaurant, Engine Company No. 3, he was looking for a farm to supply the eggs for the new breakfast and brunch restaurant in Milwaukee. The business allowed Michael's flock to expand from twenty-five chickens to six hundred.

Mama D's followed suit as owner Diana Markus sought out a sustainable source for the eggs for her cafés in Wales and Waukesha. Many others followed, including Chef Karen Bell at Bavette La Boucherie in Milwaukee, Chef Andrew Schneider of Le Rêve Patisserie & Café, and more.

Today, the farm is a primary producer of eggs, with about half sold to local grocery stores and the other half to restaurants. Their eggs are also distributed through community-supported agriculture programs at other local farms including Turtle Creek, Three Sisters, Farm Happy, and Gwenyn Hill Farms.

In addition to day-to-day farming operations, the Gutschenritters spend time stewarding their land, maintaining twenty-eight acres of warm-season grasses and pollinator mix acquired through a program of the Bee and Butterfly Habitat Fund two years ago. In 2022, their family—including their three-year-old daughter—planted over two hundred oak trees on their land. Courtney emphasizes that farming, for them, is a

higher purpose. It's about taking care of the land and producing healthful food for the community. In the case of their children, it's about raising them to be a part of something larger than themselves and to work for the greater good of those around them.

Chocolate Mousse

Chef Andrew Schneider, Le Rêve Patisserie & Café
with eggs from Three Brothers Farm

Chef Andrew Schneider says that maintaining relationships with farms like Three Brothers is very rewarding. Getting to know the farmers allows you to understand how raising their chickens impacts the flavor of their eggs— and why those eggs cost a little more. At Le Rêve, the focus is on offering guests healthful and quality fare at an affordable price. They accomplish that goal by using local vendors who farm responsibly and deliver high-quality products.

This chocolate mousse is as classic as it gets. But the quality of ingredients, from the milk and eggs to the dark chocolate, makes a huge difference in the final product. So use the best you can afford.

SERVES 4-6

For the mousse:

1 cup Wisconsin whole milk

2 cups (11 ounces) dark chocolate, chopped

8 egg yolks

1¼ cups pure cane sugar

2 cups Wisconsin heavy cream, whipped to soft peaks

For the garnish:

whipped cream

seasonal fruit

Bring milk to a boil and pour over chopped chocolate in a mixing bowl. Whisk from the center outward to emulsify, making a ganache. Set aside.

Using a double boiler (pot of simmering water with a stand mixer bowl on top), combine yolks and sugar together in the mixer bowl until sugar granules dissolve and mixture is slightly hot to touch. Remove bowl from heat, and attach to mixer with a whisk attachment. Whip on high speed until double in size and room temperature.

Fold whipped egg mixture into the chocolate ganache, and then incorporate the whipped cream in two batches, folding gently to avoid deflation. Cover the bowl with plastic wrap, pressing the wrap down onto the surface of the mousse. Chill the mousse for a minimum of 2 hours or up to a day in the refrigerator.

Spoon into glasses, and serve with more freshly whipped cream and seasonal fruit.

Hyline Orchard

Fish Creek, Wisconsin
hylineorchards.com

Door County produces 95 percent of all tart cherries grown in Wisconsin and 10 percent of the tart cherries in the United States. In fact, the twenty-five hundred orchards on the seventy-mile-long peninsula produce approximately eight to ten million pounds of cherries annually.

Among them is Hyline Orchard, a two-hundred-acre family-owned orchard that is planted with 150 acres of cherries, 30 acres of apples, and a grove of maple trees tapped seasonally for maple syrup.

The orchard was founded in 1958 by Marvin and Loretta Robertoy, who started by selling their produce along the roadside, first at a card table and then from a wagon. Eventually they converted an old machine shed on the property into a roadside market where they sold fresh fruit along with a variety of housemade items, including Loretta's homemade pies.

In time, the Robertoys' son, Paul Sr., and his wife, Vicky, joined other family members in helping to tend the orchards and harvest the fruit. When Loretta passed away in 2020, her daughter, Cindy Enigl, assumed the role of piemaker, using Loretta's recipes to fill the bakery case with fruit pies during the summer months and crafting seasonal caramel apples to sell when apples are at their peak in the autumn.

While visitors will still find Marvin, now eighty-five, tinkering and making repairs around the orchard, full operations for the orchard and market now rest with his grandchildren, Tracy and Paul Robertoy and their cousins Justin Enigl, Nathan Delsart, and Megan Delsart. Some handle the processing of housemade items including jams, jellies, pie filling, canned fruit, salsa, honey, fruit sauces, and other items to sell at the market. Others handle various aspects of the orchards, including the pick-your-own cherries, raspberries, and apples.

In addition to market sales, Hyline Orchard sells a fair number of cherries to restaurants in Wisconsin and beyond, with distributors delivering cherries throughout the Midwest. Local deliveries are also made by family to a variety of Door County restaurants, including the Harbor Fish Market and Grille, Pink Bakery, The Old Post Office Restaurant, and Not Licked Yet frozen custard.

HYLINE ORCHARD

SmallPie's Door County Hand Pies

Chief Pie Officer Valeri Lucks, SmallPie
with cherries from Hyline Orchard

This is the perfect recipe to make when Door County cherries are at their peak in July and August. These hand pies are easy to assemble and easily transportable for pot-lucks and picnics. The classic Montmorency cherries offer a classic cherry pie flavor, and the hint of cinnamon makes the filling pop.

MAKES 8 HAND PIES

For the dough:

2½ cups all-purpose flour

1 teaspoon kosher salt

1 cup unsalted, Wisconsin butter (very cold)

½ cup ice water

1 egg, room temp, beaten for egg wash (right before baking)

white sugar for finishing

For the filling:

4 cups tart red Door County cherries, pitted, fresh, or frozen

¾ cup sugar

2 tablespoons cornstarch

1 tablespoon all-purpose flour

½ teaspoon kosher salt

⅛ teaspoon cinnamon

To prepare the dough:

In a large bowl whisk together flour and salt. Add the cold butter. Using a pastry cutter or a fork, cut the butter into the flour until the mixture resembles pea-sized (but differently sized) pieces. Sprinkle 3 tablespoons of ice water over the flour mixture. Using a rubber scraper, lightly mix the flour and the water together. Add the water 3 tablespoons at a time until the dough comes together. Stop adding water as soon as the dough sticks together enough to form a ball.

Using your hands, form two balls of dough. Be careful not to overhandle the dough. Wrap the dough balls in plastic wrap and allow to rest for at least 30 minutes (up to 24 hours).

To prepare the filling:

Thaw and drain cherries very well if they are frozen. Mix all filling ingredients together in a large bowl. Set the bowl aside in the fridge.

To prepare the hand pies:

Reheat the oven to 400°F.

Remove the dough from the fridge. Divide dough into eight equally sized balls of dough. On a well-floured surface, roll out one ball of dough to a 7-inch diameter circle. It's OK if it's not perfect. Keep the rest of the dough refrigerated as you roll all the dough out. Place circles back in the fridge as you roll the rest of the dough.

Take one circle of dough and place it on a lined baking sheet. Scoop about ½ cup of the cherry mixture into the center. Fold up edges of dough around and over cherry filling— this step may be a bit messy. Alternatively, you can fold the dough around four times so you have a little "square" or you can fold the dough around the filling in five folds so you have

SMALLPIE

a circle-ish shape. You may also put the dough into a large (Texas-size) muffin tin cup and scoop the filling in there, folding the dough over the top. The muffin tin helps to contain the juicy cherries.

Repeat until all the dough is used. Freeze prepped pies on a baking sheet for 30 minutes to firm up the dough.

Whisk the egg and brush over the top of the pies. Bake the pies for 45–55 minutes. When the crust is browned and the filling is bubbly through the top opening, remove from the oven. Dust the tops with white sugar immediately. Use as much or as little sugar as you like.

Allow to cool for at least 2 hours before eating so the filling can finish "cooking"—it needs time out of the oven to set up. You can rewarm the pies after they have fully cooled.

Honeypie Cafe's Chocolate Cream Pie

Chief Pie Officer Valeri Lucks, Honeypie Cafe
with milk from Sassy Cow Creamery

Silky, chocolatey, and easy as pie (pun intended). That's the chocolate cream pie from Honeypie Cafe. This crowd pleaser is among their most popular offerings for very good reason. It's also a breeze to make. Secrets include using high-quality dairy and the highest-quality chocolate you can afford.

SERVES 8

For the crust:

1½ cups graham cracker crumbs, finely ground

½ cup sugar

½ teaspoon kosher salt

8 tablespoons butter, melted

For the filling:

4 egg yolks

½ teaspoon kosher salt

½ cup sugar

¼ cup cornstarch

2½ cups whole milk

1 tablespoon vanilla

1 cup chopped dark chocolate or chocolate chips (60–70 percent dark chocolate)

For the garnish:

2 cups heavy whipping cream, whipped to soft peaks

chocolate chips or shaved dark chocolate

To prepare the crust:

Preheat the oven to 350°F.

Whisk dry ingredients together in a large bowl. Pour the melted butter over the graham mixture. Stir together until butter is incorporated (mixture should feel like wet sand). Press graham mixture into a deep 9-inch pie pan. Use the bottom of a glass or a measuring cup to press the crust together firmly in the pan. Bake for 8 minutes. Cool completely before filling.

To prepare the filling:

In a large nonreactive saucepan, whisk together the egg yolks, salt, and sugar until glossy and a pale yellow color. Slowly whisk in cornstarch until smooth and glossy. Pour in half of the milk and whisk together. Pour in the other half of the milk and whisk together. Put the pan over medium-high heat, whisk very slowly but constantly and cook until bubbles form and the mixture is thickened (about 10 minutes). Remove from heat and add the vanilla. Mix the chocolate into the hot filling. Whisk until all the chocolate has melted.

Pour the chocolate mixture over the bottom of the cooled pie crust. Cover with plastic wrap and refrigerate 4 hours until cool. Top with whipped cream and decorate pie with some shaved chocolate or chocolate chips.

Whipping Cream Like a Pro

Most home cooks beat their whipped cream at high speed. That method definitely works. However, when you take the time to whip it at medium speed, the cream transforms into a stable matrix of fat, water, and air. There's no stability when you whip cream on high. You get too many differently sized molecules. However, at medium speed all the bubbles are the same size, giving you a far better whipped cream that will remain light and fluffy for longer.

JESS BURNS

Pink Teepee Farms / Sourced in Nature

Ottawa, Wisconsin
pinkteepeefarms.com
sinfoods.com

In 2015, Molly and Ben Wiedenman decided to take a leap and establish their own farm. Molly had formerly worked as a teacher and Ben had gone to school for environmental science, working in aquaponics and aquaculture for Growing Power and as a researcher at the School of Freshwater Sciences at the University of Wisconsin–Milwaukee. They'd always grown organic produce in their home garden, but they wanted to take their passion a step further. From there, Pink Teepee Farms was born.

During their first season, the couple took on side hustles to make ends meet and launched a CSA program. Sales were mostly to friends and family who wanted to support their nascent efforts, but the support gave them a sense of how they wanted to operate. They picked up business from a few restaurants as they moved forward, and by 2021 they decided to refocus their efforts on growing premium items for local chefs.

Pink Teepee was created as an intentionally small operation. Situated on three acres of land, with one acre dedicated to farming, the farm is optimized by succession planting and crop rotation, both practices that assist in controlling pests and diseases. Although they are not certified as an organic farm, the couple is dedicated to the use of organic practices, taking pride in going above and beyond the USDA guidelines. They've also focused their efforts on permaculture, expanding perennial crops like pears, apples, plums, cherries, rhubarb, and horseradish and saving seeds for use from year to year.

In time, foraging also became part of their model. In 2018, they increased the efficiency of their operations by partnering with Bryan De Stefanis, a forager and farmer who owns property and operates a farm in Tigerton, Wisconsin. Together, they pulled together the foraging end of the business—along with a line of products like maple syrup, honey, and other chef-driven shelf-stable products made with local ingredients—under the "Sourced in Nature" moniker, giving both farms an additional revenue stream.

JESS BURNS

Molly says Pink Teepee's work with restaurants often begins in the off-season when they sit down with chefs to plan the crops they might grow that year. As the season progresses, they offer a weekly menu of seasonal items to each of their restaurant customers.

Belfrē Kitchen was the first restaurant the farm worked with, and they've continued to be loyal customers, assisting the farm in developing their plans for future crops and foraged items. Being able to work synergistically with local restaurant partners has not only assisted them in growing their farm's business but also given them a consistent sense of satisfaction knowing that their produce is being used in dishes that can be enjoyed by so many members of the public.

Pink Teepee Farms is built on relationships. From the farmers' relationships with Mother Nature to the relationships they've built with restaurants and market customers, it's the synergy between the soil, the trees, and the human beings that drives them forward.

Carrot Snack Cake with Maple Citrus Glaze

Pastry Chef Annelise Linton, Belfrē Kitchen
with carrots from Jerry's Produce and syrup from Sourced in Nature

Carrot cake is a classic and comforting dessert. It can be simple or it can be dressed up in many fun ways. This recipe is a hybrid of favorite recipes made over the years, resulting in a moist cake with a few twists that still embodies what a classic carrot cake should be.

The exceptional carrots from Jerry's Produce lend a beautiful electric orange color to this cake, and while there's no pineapple, the coriander—along with that bit of additional sweetness in the carrots—offers a bit of that fruity flavor. The maple syrup, which comes from Pink Teepee Farms / Sourced in Nature is available in a range of varieties; each one will offer a slightly different flavor to this recipe. The lemon in the glaze offers this cake an overall lift and lightness that keeps it from feeling too heavy.

SERVES 8-10

For the cake:

2 eggs

¾ cup plus 2 tablespoons light brown sugar

¼ cup plus 3 tablespoons canola oil

1½ cups all-purpose flour

¼ teaspoon baking soda

1½ teaspoons baking powder

1 teaspoon cinnamon

½ teaspoon coriander

¾ teaspoon kosher salt

½ cup chopped walnuts (optional)

1 cup carrots, washed, peeled, and grated

¼ cup plus 1 tablespoon Greek yogurt

To prepare the cake:

Preheat the oven to 350°F and place a rack in the center of the oven.

Trace a circular piece of parchment using your cake pan. Cut two additional strips of parchment that are about 12 inches long. Spray the bottom of your pan and place parchment strips in an X shape on the very bottom, making sure the ends hang out over the sides. Place the parchment circle over the strips, pressing down to ensure that it's flush, and spray the bottom and sides lightly with cooking spray.

In a mixing bowl (you can use a stand mixer if you have one), combine the eggs and brown sugar and whisk until light in color and smooth (about 2–3 minutes). Add in the oil and whisk, scraping down the sides halfway through mixing. Continue to mix until the mixture no longer looks clumpy or separated but smooth and well combined.

In a separate bowl, combine flour, baking soda, baking powder, cinnamon, coriander, and salt, and whisk until smooth and any lumps are broken apart. If you're using walnuts, toss them in with the flour mixture to evenly coat. Set aside.

For the glaze:

zest of 1 lemon

1 cup powdered sugar

¼ teaspoon kosher salt

3 tablespoons maple syrup

¼ teaspoon maple extract

1 tablespoon plus ½ teaspoon milk

Into the egg and sugar mixture, add the Greek yogurt and whisk until smooth. Add carrots and fold in until carrots are well coated. Add the dry ingredients to the carrot mixture and stir until just combined and no bits of flour or dry ingredients remain. The batter will be on the thick side. Pour the batter into the prepared cake pan and tap twice on the table top to remove any air bubbles and allow mixture to settle evenly into pan.

Bake for about 15 minutes and rotate 180 degrees. Continue baking an additional 15–20 minutes until the cake bounces back in the center when lightly pressed or a cake tester inserted into the middle comes out clean. Remove from the oven and cool on a rack, in the pan, for about 10 minutes, and then grab the ends of the parchment strips and lift the cake out of the pan and place on the rack to cool completely.

To prepare the glaze:

While the cake is cooling, make your glaze. Finely zest one lemon. In a small bowl, whisk together lemon zest, powdered sugar, and salt. Add in the maple syrup, maple extract, and milk. You can adjust the consistency by adding a touch more milk if needed. Once the cake is cool, pour the glaze over the top, allowing it to run down the sides.

Allow the cake to set for a few minutes before slicing and serving. Cake can be stored at room temperature or kept in the fridge, well wrapped, for up to three days.

Strawberry-Rhubarb Tres Leches Cake

Chefs Paul Zerkel and Lisa Kirkpatrick, Goodkind with fruit from Baby Mama Botanicals

This fruity take on the traditional tres leches cake is sweet, tart, and deceptively complex thanks to the custard-like consistency created through soaking. Chef Lisa Kirkpatrick at Goodkind uses it to make use of early season fruit from Baby Mama Botanicals. But this cake is easy to modify using different types of fruit, so it can be enjoyed year-round.

MAKES ONE 9 X 13 INCH CAKE

SERVES 12–15

For the cake:

12 tablespoons unsalted butter, at room temperature

1½ cups toasted granulated sugar

7 large eggs

1½ teaspoons vanilla extract

2¼ cups all-purpose flour

1½ teaspoons baking powder

¾ teaspoon fine sea salt

For the soaking liquid:

2 cups strawberries, sliced

2 cups rhubarb, sliced

⅓ cup granulated sugar

½ vanilla bean, scraped

½ cup whole milk

1¾ cups whipping cream

1½ cups goat's milk

To prepare the cake:

Preheat the oven to 350°F.

Lightly grease a 9 × 13 inch pan with cooking spray. In the bowl of an electric mixer, cream the butter and sugar until light and fluffy (about 4–5 minutes). Add the eggs one at a time, mixing well to combine. Stir in the vanilla.

In a medium bowl, whisk the flour, baking powder, and salt together. Add the flour mixture to the butter and mix just until incorporated. Be sure to scrape down the sides to ensure that the batter is evenly mixed.

Pour the batter into the prepared baking pan and bake until a toothpick inserted into the center comes out clean (about 38–40 minutes). Allow the cake to cool completely before proceeding.

Once the cake is cool, poke holes all over with a wooden skewer. Stir together the strawberries, rhubarb, sugar, and vanilla bean scrapings in a medium-size pot and bring to a simmer over medium heat. Simmer for about 15 minutes or until the fruit is very soft but not fully broken down.

Strain the mixture, pressing lightly on the fruit solids to release the juices but not enough to push the solids through the sieve. Measure the liquid after straining. You should have about ¾ cup. If you have more, return it to the stove and reduce it slightly by simmering over medium heat until a portion of the liquid evaporates. If you have less, add a bit of water to make up the difference and stir to combine.

Whisk together the strawberry-rhubarb syrup, milk, whipping cream, and goat's milk in a large pitcher. Gently

For the chèvre whipped cream:

4 tablespoons fresh chèvre (goat cheese)

1 cup heavy cream

2 tablespoons sugar

For the garnish:

additional fresh strawberries

pour the mixture evenly all over the cake, allowing it to seep through the holes and soak into the cake. Allow the cake to rest for about 30 minutes until the mixture is absorbed.

To prepare the chèvre whipped cream:

Place the chèvre in a small bowl and stir in a bit of heavy cream just to soften it. Set aside.

In a medium bowl, using a whisk or an electric mixer, whip the remaining heavy cream until soft peaks form. Slowly add the sugar and chèvre to the cream just until medium peaks begin to form again. Use immediately.

After the cake has soaked up the milk mixture, top the cake with chèvre whipped cream and fresh strawberries. Serve immediately. You can also refrigerate the finished cake for up to 5 hours before serving.

Toasted Sugar

You might think it's crazy to go through the trouble of caramelizing sugar, but the reward is granulated sugar that tastes like caramel. It can be used exactly like regular granulated sugar in any recipe, and it flawlessly transforms buttercream frosting, cheesecake, and even your morning oatmeal into something special. Since the process is somewhat lengthy, it's worthwhile to do a whole 4-pound bag of sugar at once. I guarantee you'll easily find ways to use the sugar.

Preheat oven to 325°F.

Pour the 4-pound bag of granulated white sugar into a glass or ceramic 9 × 13 inch pan, shaking it to form an even layer. (Do not use a metal pan; it will cause the sugar to melt.) Place the pan on the middle rack of your preheated oven. Toast the sugar for 4 hours, stirring it every 30 minutes to release the steam from the sugar and break up any clumps that have formed. Take care to move the sugar at the edges of the pan toward the middle to ensure even heat distribution.

After 4 hours, the sugar will have taken on a caramel color and the flavor will be deep and caramelly with notes of vanilla. Cool the sugar thoroughly and store in an airtight, sealed container. Use it in any recipe that calls for granulated sugar.

Carrot Cake with Peach and Ginger Cream Cheese Frosting and Candied Heirloom Carrots

Pastry Chef Jonna Zaczek, Third Coast Provisions, Merriment Social, and Flourchild Pizza
with carrots and peaches from Centgraf Farms

When it comes to desserts, Pastry Chef Jonna Zaczek is a master at fashioning creative new offerings that are solidly nostalgic. This carrot cake offers all the comfort of the classic, with a lovely summer twist thanks to peach and ginger cream cheese frosting. The rustic candied heirloom carrots that decorate the top are a pleasantly sweet surprise.

MAKES ONE 9-INCH THREE-LAYER CAKE

SERVES 15

For the candied heirloom carrots:

1 cup sugar

1 cup water

4–5 heirloom carrots, shaved with peeler

For the cake:

1 cup sunflower oil

2 cups sugar

4 large eggs

1 teaspoon vanilla paste (1½ teaspoons if using vanilla extract)

2½ cups all-purpose flour

1 tablespoon plus 2 teaspoons cinnamon

1 tablespoon baking soda

½ teaspoon kosher salt

1 cup buttermilk

2 medium carrots, peeled and shredded

For the peach compote:

2 medium to large peaches, small diced

¾ cup sugar

1 teaspoon vanilla

1 tablespoon lemon juice

pinch of cinnamon

For the frosting:

½ pound unsalted butter, softened

2 pounds cream cheese, softened

½ cup peach compote

1 teaspoon finely grated/minced fresh ginger

1 tablespoon vanilla paste (1½ tablespoons if using vanilla extract)

To prepare the candied carrots:

Combine sugar and water in a pot and bring to a boil. Add carrots and boil for about 1 minute. If you are using any purple carrots, do those separately; otherwise, everything will be discolored. Remove carrots from boiling syrup and place in a small container in the refrigerator until needed.

To prepare the cake:

Preheat the oven to 350°F.

Spray three 9-inch cake pans with pan spray. In the bowl of a mixer fitted with a paddle, place oil and sugar and stir on low until combined. Add eggs and vanilla and mix until all the eggs are fully incorporated.

Sift flour, cinnamon, and baking soda into a bowl. Add salt to dry ingredients. Alternate adding sifted dry ingredients and buttermilk to the mixing bowl and stir on low for a few seconds between additions until everything is incorporated and you have a smooth cake batter.

Remove bowl from mixer; add the shredded carrots to the bowl and give them a good stir.

Divide batter evenly between your three prepared pans and then bake in oven for approximately 15–20 minutes (or until a cake tester comes out clean).

Once baked, remove from the oven and let the cakes cool in the pans at room temperature. When the pans are cool enough to touch, you can flip your cakes out onto a cooling rack.

While waiting for the cakes to cool, prepare the peach compote and the frosting.

To prepare the peach compote:

Place diced peaches in a sauté pan with all the other ingredients. Cook on medium low until the peaches are fully cooked and jammy. Remove from heat and allow to cool so that it can be incorporated into the cream cheese frosting.

To prepare the frosting:

Place butter and cream cheese in the bowl of a mixer fitted with the paddle attachment and mix on medium speed until combined and no lumps remain. Scrape down the sides of the bowl well, and then add the remaining ingredients. Mix on medium speed for about 30 seconds to combine.

To frost the cakes:

Start by leveling out the cakes. Do this by simply lopping off the hump in the middle, but you can be as precise as you want. The top you slice off makes for a great snack to tide you over while waiting for the final product.

Once the cakes are leveled, drop a quarter of your frosting on the bottom cake and smooth over the top. Make sure you're going all the way to the edges. Repeat this step for the next layer. When you get to the third cake, start smoothing a thin layer of frosting around the sides and top of all the cakes to seal in the crumbs. Once you have your thin layer, you can go right over with a thick layer of frosting. There should be enough frosting left to get a nice even coat on the entire cake.

The last step is adding candied carrot ribbons. It's fine to haphazardly place them along the outside of the top of the cake. If the carrots are still wet with simple syrup, you can pat them dry on a paper towel.

Gluten-Free Carrot Cake Cupcakes

Chef Michael Fifarek, Parkside 23
with carrots from Parkside 23 Farm

It's a goal at Parkside 23 to offer as many gluten-free dishes as possible to accommodate guests. It's also a goal to make them just as delicious as the original recipes. These cupcakes are a great example. The recipe incorporates farm carrots, raisins, nuts, and coconut to create a classic carrot cake profile that doesn't contain any gluten.

MAKES 8–10 CUPCAKES

For the cupcakes:

1 cup plus 2⅓ tablespoons (5½ ounces) Bob's Red Mill gluten-free flour

1 teaspoon baking soda

¼ teaspoon xanthan gum

½ teaspoon kosher salt

¾ cup canola oil

1 cup granulated sugar

2 eggs

2 cups shredded carrots

⅓ cup shredded coconut

2 ounces raisins

¼ cup pecans, chopped

For the cream cheese frosting:

8 ounces cream cheese at room temperature

4 ounces butter at room temperature

2 cups powdered sugar

To prepare the cupcakes:

Preheat the oven to 350°F.

Combine flour, baking soda, xanthan gum, and salt in a medium bowl and mix well.

In a large bowl, combine oil and sugar and mix well with an electric mixer. Add eggs one at a time, incorporating each on low speed. Add the dry ingredients to the egg and sugar mixture, and mix well. Stir in remaining ingredients.

Using classic muffin pan with cupcake paper liners, scoop about 3 ounces of batter into each cup (liners should be about ¾ full). Place the pan in the oven and bake for about 10–12 minutes. Rotate cupcakes and continue to bake for about another 10–12 minutes. Once cupcakes are done, remove from oven and place on cooling rack.

To prepare the frosting:

While the cupcakes are cooling, prepare the frosting. Place the cream cheese and butter in a medium-size bowl and mix well using an electric mixer. Mix in sugar until completely incorporated, with a frosting consistency. Place frosting in a pastry bag with a star tip, or you can spread using a butter knife. Once cupcakes have cooled to room temperature, frost each cupcake with your desired amount of frosting.

Meadowlark Organics

Ridgeway, Wisconsin
meadowlarkorganics.com

After years of working in the restaurant industry in New York, Halee and John Wepking came to a crossroads in their careers. It was 2014, and they found themselves on a hunt for farmland in Wisconsin. Together they decided to move back to John's home state and pursue meaningful food-related work that would make a tangible difference in the world: farming seemed to be the answer.

Initially, they found work running a breakfast and lunch restaurant in Lancaster, Wisconsin. But they spent their weekends working on John's family's farm and keeping their eyes open for opportunities to purchase land for a farm of their own.

When Halee happened upon a Craigslist post from Paul Bickford, a longtime farmer in Ridgeway, Wisconsin, who was looking for an ambitious young person he could train to take over his farm, she wrote him a very enthusiastic email. He replied favorably. After meeting the aspiring farmers, he hired them to work on the farm and assist him in forming a succession plan. By 2020, Halee and John were co-owners of the farm, which they currently run jointly with Paul and his son Levi.

The farm, which began as a three-hundred-cow dairy farm in 1978, became a leader in rotational grazing during the 1990s before Paul sold the cows and converted 950 acres of land to grain production. When the Wepkings joined the farm, they took the time to learn the ropes. But as they moved forward, they also focused their energy on enhancements, including expanding the diversity of crops grown, as well as improving cleaning, storage, and postharvest handling of their grains.

Meadowlark Organics operates under the guidelines of USDA Organic certification, but also relies on practices that preserve the farm's ecosystem and the integrity of the land. Crops include corn, alfalfa, and oats, along with spring and winter wheat, spelt, einkorn, and up to 150 acres of buckwheat, most of which serves as a cover crop as well as a destination for beekeepers seeking the fragrant August blooms for their honey production. The farm has also branched out into growing popcorn and dried beans.

More recently, they've begun milling their own grains. For years, Meadowlark Organics worked with Gilbert Williams, co-owner of Lonesome Stone Milling in Lone Rock, Wisconsin, to mill their grains, enabling them to sell flour and other products directly to wholesale bakers and at farmers markets. But in 2021, when Gilbert decided to retire, they

purchased his equipment and rebuilt the mill right on their farm. Around the same time, they purchased two additional New American Stone Mills from Vermont with the goal of improving the quality and consistency of their grains and flours, particularly bread flour.

Meadowlark takes great pride in the quality of its freshly milled grains. They've been surprised and delighted by the amount of flavor they've been able to coax from their products, largely due to the care they take in the growth, harvesting, storage, and processing of their grain. The quality has earned them a loyal customer base through their online store, their one-hundred-member CSA program, and an increasing number of wholesale accounts, including the Willy Street Coop in Madison, Metcalfe Market in Madison and Milwaukee, and Outpost Natural Foods.

The clean, fresh flavor of their product has also been a selling point for restaurants, most of which have connected with the farm and mill through word of mouth. Current accounts include numerous bakeries in Madison along with Milwaukee restaurants such as Birch, Bavette La Boucherie, and Pizza Man, which committed to using 100 percent Meadowlark Organic Flour in their thin crust pizzas in 2021.

Having worked in restaurants themselves, the Wepkings note that it's been vital to cultivate personal relationships with restaurants and bakeries and put products into the hands of people like Chef Francesca Hong of Morris Ramen, who has helped to tell the story of the farm by showcasing the quality of their products in her restaurant dishes.

But, overall, Halee says that she and John find a great deal of satisfaction in growing food products and processing flour that is connected to a larger local agricultural movement. And even though a thousand acres is just a small parcel in the grand scheme of things, there's security and comfort in knowing that the farm is a direct line to nature and has an impact on the environment and the food system on the whole.

She can't emphasize enough the power that home cooks can have on the food system, especially for small operations like Meadowlark. While restaurants can't always afford to purchase from small local businesses—in many cases due to slim profit margins—converting a home pantry to all local flour is a relatively small investment.

Burnt Honey Bourbon Cake

Chef Francesca Hong, Morris Ramen
with spelt flour from Meadowlark Organics

If you are looking for a crowd-pleasing cake that's complex in flavor but not too sweet, this one is the perfect solution. Buttermilk and sunflower oil ensure a moist crumb, while heating the honey to its smoking point before use adds caramel notes and a pleasant complexity.

You can make this cake in an 8-inch square or round pan. It also makes a beautiful Bundt cake.

LORI FREDRICH

SERVES 10-12

For the cake:

1 cup local honey

¼ cup plus 2 teaspoons J. Henry Bourbon

2½ cups spelt flour

2 teaspoons kosher salt

¾ teaspoon baking soda

1 cup sunflower oil

¾ cup plus 1 tablespoon buttermilk

3 eggs

For the topping:

2 cups heavy cream

fresh fruit (optional)

orange zest (optional)

To prepare the cake:

Preheat the oven to 325°F.

Grease and flour your cake pan of choice. Pour the honey into a heavy-bottomed sauté pan. Heat over medium-high heat until you see smoke. This process will take 3–5 minutes. The honey will bubble and steam as it heats, but you want to wait until it begins to darken and smoke. Turn off the heat immediately, drizzle in the bourbon, and allow to cool. Be careful, as the bourbon will cause the honey to sizzle up in the pan.

Sift and whisk together flour, salt, and baking soda into a bowl. In a separate bowl, whisk together the honey and bourbon mixture, sunflower oil, buttermilk, and eggs. Add the dry ingredients to the wet ingredients. Whisk to combine, but do not overmix. Pour the batter into the prepared pan. Bake for 35–40 minutes or until a cake tester comes out moist but clean. Allow to cool before serving.

To prepare the topping:

About 20 minutes before you'd like to serve the cake, place the bowl and whisk from your electric mixer into the freezer to get them as cold as possible. When the bowl has chilled, pour cold heavy cream into the bowl and whisk at medium speed until stiff peaks form.

You can spread the whipped cream over the entire cake or serve slices of the cake with a dollop of cream. Add fresh fruit or orange zest, if desired.

Local Libations

Recipes

Featured Producers

Sweet Corn Old Fashioned

Katie Rose, Goodkind
with corn from Centgraf Farms

The Old Fashioned is a Wisconsin classic. In fact, the Dairy State even has its own version of the classic cocktail, which is served in taverns throughout the state. This is not that cocktail. But it's a worthy homage to a state that's known for its delicious sweet corn.

In this super summery riff, fresh sweet corn is infused into bourbon. Feel free to eat the kernels of corn you remove from the corn cobs; they're not necessary for the infusion. But be sure to save all the juicy bits of the cob to put into the spirits.

Browning butter can be tricky. It takes a bit of patience, and you cannot walk away or it's guaranteed to burn. But don't let that discourage you. Use a stainless-steel pan so that you can see the color change in the butter more easily and watch it closely. Your nose will tell you when the butter is getting close; it smells amazingly nutty and wonderful.

This recipe makes a liter of both brown butter and sweet corn bourbon, but you won't be sorry. Both are delicious and can be used for other cocktails or cooking. They are amazing in a summery bourbon caramel sauce.

MAKES 1 COCKTAIL

PLUS 1 LITER EACH OF BROWN BUTTER AND SWEET CORN BOURBON

For the sweet corn-infused bourbon:

1-4 ears of fresh sweet corn, kernels removed (depending on how much corn flavor you want)

1 liter bourbon

For the brown butter bourbon:

8 tablespoons butter

1 liter bourbon

To prepare the sweet corn–infused bourbon:

Place the juicy corn cobs in a large jar or other sealable container. Pour bourbon over the cobs, making sure the bourbon is covering the entirety of the cobs, and let them sit for five to seven days. You can taste the bourbon after five days to see how it's doing. It will have a distinctly corn-like flavor. After the desired taste is achieved, remove cobs and strain bourbon through cheesecloth to eliminate any debris. Rebottle the bourbon in a clean sealable container and label appropriately.

To prepare the brown butter bourbon:

Place the butter in a medium saucepan over medium-high heat. Melt it completely and then lower flame to medium, swirling the pan as you go. Simmer the butter, swirling occasionally until a foam develops. This development means you're getting close. When the butter begins to foam a second time, you'll see it turning a golden brown. You'll also smell it as it caramelizes. Once this golden brown

ALIZA BARAN

For the drink:

2 ounces sweet corn–
infused bourbon

¼ ounces simple syrup

1 dash Angostura
bitters

1 dash Bittercube
Orange bitters

1 bar spoon brown
butter bourbon

orange peel, for garnish

large ice cube

color is achieved, remove from heat and let it cool to room temperature.

Put your bourbon in a clean glass jar. Then add the cooled brown butter to the bourbon. There's no need to shake it. Seal the jar and put it in the freezer for two to three days. When the bourbon is frozen, the butter will form a fat cap at the top of the jar. To strain, puncture the fat cap and pour the brown butter bourbon through a double-lined cheesecloth strainer. Rebottle your strained brown butter bourbon into a clean jar and store in the fridge.

To prepare the drink:

Place all ingredients in a stirring vessel. Add ice and stir briskly until well chilled. Strain into a rocks glass with a large format ice cube. Garnish with orange peel.

Siren Shrub Co.

Stevens Point, Wisconsin
sirenshrubs.com

It was a fateful day in 2015 when Layne Cozzolino and Mindy McCord stumbled on a recipe for a shrub, a vinegar-and-fruit-based beverage that had its heyday in the 1800s when folks needed ways to preserve their fruit without refrigeration. Intrigued, they began making their own.

The following summer, when Layne found out she was pregnant, the idea of shrubs took on new meaning as the two friends discovered that they were the perfect substitute for alcoholic beverages. As they tested their recipes at farmers markets and gatherings, they noticed that the drinks appealed to a wide variety of people and were perfect for drinking on their own with sparkling water or as an ingredient in craft cocktails and mocktails.

SIREN SHRUB CO.

They started their woman-owned beverage brand, Siren Shrub Company, as a side hustle, creating shrubs with natural ingredients like apple cider vinegar, fresh fruits, roots, and herbs, sweetened with cane sugar or maple syrup.

Each bottled shrub is based on ingredients from a local Wisconsin-based farm. Honeycrisp uses apples from The Glass Orchard in Eau Claire; Lemongrass and Basil use herbs from Whitefeather Organics in Custer; Tart Cherry uses Montmorency cherries from Seaquist Orchards in Door County; and Maple Ginger uses maple syrup from Tapped Maple Syrup in Stevens Point.

Today, Siren Shrub manufactures six bottled shrubs and four canned sparkling beverages (basil, tart cherry, coffee, and Honeycrisp). Their products are available for purchase on their website as well as countless locations across the United States. The shrubs have gained the attention of numerous notable Wisconsin mixologists and are served in restaurants throughout Wisconsin, including Bavette La Boucherie and Saffron in Milwaukee, Ruby Cafe in Stevens Point, and Trixie's in Door County.

Watermelon Punch

Mindy McCord, Siren Shrub Co.

Is there anything better than biting into a perfectly sweet and juicy piece of watermelon at peak season? Perhaps this watermelon punch. It's a cocktail so juicy and refreshing that you'll be making it on repeat all summer long. The Lemongrass Siren Shrub in this recipe features lemongrass grown by Whitefeather Organics in Custer, Wisconsin.

SERVES 6

For watermelon juice:

1 large (6-7 pound) watermelon

For the punch:

6 cups of watermelon juice

¾ cup lemon juice

¼ cup lime juice

¼ cup orange juice

1 cup tequila (optional)

4 ounces Lemongrass Siren Shrub

pinch of kosher salt

To prepare the watermelon juice:

Cut six small triangles from a slice of a large (6-7 pounds) watermelon and reserve for garnish. Cut the remaining watermelon into chunks with the rind and seeds removed. Put the watermelon chunks into a blender and blend until liquid. Drape a cheesecloth over a strainer with a bowl below and pour the watermelon juice onto the cheesecloth. Discard or compost pulp solids remaining in the strainer.

To prepare the punch:

Whisk all of the ingredients in a large pitcher or punch bowl. Add ice when ready to serve. Garnish each glass with a reserved watermelon triangle.

SIREN SHRUB CO.

Cool as a Cucumber

Mindy McCord, Siren Shrub Co.

A cocktail that is complex but not complicated, this quaff will fill your glass with summer and cool you down with an abundance of fresh balanced flavor. It's best enjoyed with your feet up outside on the patio. The Tart Cherry Siren Shrub in the drink is made with cherries grown at Seaquist Orchards in Door County, Wisconsin.

MAKES 1 COCKTAIL

- 4 slices of cucumber
- 3 fresh basil leaves
- 2 fresh sprigs of mint, plus an extra sprig for garnish
- 1½ ounces fresh squeezed lemon juice
- 1 ounce Siren Shrub Tart Cherry
- 1½ ounces gin (optional)
- 2 ounces sparkling water
- 2 ounces tonic water

In a shaker, muddle the cucumber, basil, mint, lemon juice, shrub, and the optional gin. Add ice to the shaker and shake vigorously for 30 seconds. Strain into a glass with ice, and top with sparkling and tonic water. Stir to combine and garnish with a sprig of mint.

SIREN SHRUB CO.

Any Fruit Shrub

Mindy McCord, Siren Shrub Co.
with fruit of choice from your local farmers market

Before refrigeration, shrubs had a very practical use: simply, they were a way to preserve the season's bounty. The combination of vinegar, fruit, and sugar created a tasty syrup that could be enjoyed year-round. Shrubs were all the rage in the 1800s, commonly used as a syrup in public houses but versatile enough to hydrate farmers in the field.

It's no surprise that shrubs are again gaining popularity in the beverage space, loved by drinkers and nondrinkers alike. They are still versatile enough to flex between cocktails and mocktails without compromising taste. For the avid gardeners and farmers market connoisseurs, shrubs still serve the original purpose: they are a delicious way to preserve the wonders of the growing season. The Any Fruit Shrub is exactly what you imagine: grab a sack of your favorite summer fruit and try your hand at making a shrub of your own to splash into your cocktails, mocktails, desserts, and much more.

SERVES 12

1 pound unpeeled but pitted and roughly chopped fruit of choice

1 cup sugar

1 cup apple cider, balsamic, or white wine vinegar

To prepare the shrub:

Mix the fruit and sugar in a glass or other nonplastic bowl and, with a utensil, roughly break apart the fruit to bring out its juices. Cover the bowl and refrigerate for 24 hours. Afterward, stir the mixture well. Add vinegar and stir again to combine making sure sugar is fully dissolved. Using a fine sieve, strain the shrub mixture, pressing the solids to get all of the juice. Pour the mixture into a clean Mason jar or funnel into a glass bottle.

To prepare a drink:

Add 1 ounce of shrub to 6–8 ounces of sparkling water, lemonade, ice tea, or ginger beer.

Garden Gimlet

Corey Ochoa, Saffron Modern Indian Dining
with edible flowers from Baby Mama Botanicals

Creating cocktails that are new and exciting while remaining true to their classic roots is a challenge Corey Ochoa faces on a daily basis. While she loves adding twists and flare to her cocktails, she also wants them to be accessible for her customers.

For this patio-worthy cocktail, she played with different infusions and syrups to achieve a drink with distinctly fresh vegetal characteristics. Most variations were either too subtle or far too bold. Then she discovered Greenbar Garden vodka, which offered the perfect garden-esque flavor. Even better, the cocktail looks the part thanks to the basil and edible flower garnish from Baby Mama Botanicals.

MAKES 1 COCKTAIL

1 ounce fresh lime juice

1 ounce simple syrup

1 ounce Death's Door gin

1 ounce Greenbar Garden vodka

4 dashes cucumber bitters

purple basil sprig, for garnish

edible flower, for garnish

Combine all ingredients in a shaker tin, add ice, and shake vigorously. Strain into a rocks glass with fresh ice. Garnish with purple basil and edible flowers.

COREY OCHOA/SAFFRON

Parkside School for the Arts

Milwaukee, Wisconsin
www5.milwaukee.k12.wi.us/school/parkside

Gardening has been part of the curriculum at Parkside School for the Arts since 2014 when school personnel invested in the creation of native perennial gardens. But when Erin Dentice was hired on contract to create an agricultural program for the school in 2017, things picked up speed.

Erin, who had left a career in finance to return to school for community leadership and development, was hired to work alongside the Medical College of Wisconsin on a study that looked at the effects of nutrition education on students' behavior, self-efficacy, confidence, and health.

Erin, who fully realized that much of students' formal education typically revolves around test scores, says she hoped to engage them in learning that also provided practical life applications. Ultimately, the vision was to create a hands-on program that would not only exist inside the classroom but also engage students' families through programming and volunteerism.

To that end, the program utilizes arts-based cross-curricular project-based learning opportunities for students in grades K–8. These opportunities have engaged students in both the arts and agriculture through a variety of media, including the creation of murals, mud painting, and activities that integrate science, math, reading, and social studies. The program has been able to create various agricultural spaces, including an aquaponics lab, eight raised beds, two hoop houses, and plots in a nearby community garden.

The program was also built to engage with the local community, engaging

chefs, farmers, and other professionals in both educational classes and field trips. Colectivo Coffee Roasters has offered piemaking classes for students. Braise has taken students on tours of their restaurant, culinary school, and rooftop garden.

In the beginning, vegetables grown by the students as part of the agriculture program were sold to Bay View High School for use in their culinary arts program. But in 2019 the program supported the creation of a farmers market where vegetables from Parkside's gardens were sold to the public, including local restaurants.

Erin says the program has offered many takeaways, from the simple plea-sures of working in the dirt and planting things to seeing students actively engaged in field trips and knowing they could take inspiration from one of the experiences and it could shape the direction of their future.

An integral component of the agricultural program is teaching children about foodways and food cultures. Decisions about what to plant in the hoop houses are informed by the food traditions of Parkside families. Meanwhile, activities like family culinary arts nights have served to not only nourish students and their parents with seasonal, nutrient-dense meals but also engage them in learning about one another's cultures as they enjoy family recipes representing over twenty-five countries.

Sweet Pea G&T

Katie Rose, Goodkind
with sweet peas from Parkside School for the Arts

There's nothing like the taste of fresh, sweet farm-fresh peas, and this cocktail gives you a great excuse to head to the farmers market and purchase a bunch of them. Not only will you be able to snack on them for days, but you can also use the husks, which normally go to waste, to infuse your gin with amazing flavor.

Mixologist Katie Rose advises sticking with a no-frills London dry gin for this recipe, which allows the flavor of the sweet peas to shine through. When it comes to tonic water, she loves the flavor of Fever Free Indian Tonic. But locally made tonics like Top Note are also a great option.

MAKES 1 COCKTAIL

PLUS 1 LITER OF SWEET PEA GIN

For the sweet pea–infused gin:

1 quart fresh sweet pea husks

1 liter London dry gin

For the cocktail:

½ ounce fresh lemon juice

½ ounce simple syrup

½ ounce white wine (preferably Chenin Blanc, Chablis, or a Pino Grigio)

¾ ounce sweet pea–infused London dry gin

½ ounce Cocchi Americano

tonic water

For the garnish:

whole fresh sweet peas

fresh mint sprigs

To prepare the sweet pea–infused gin:

Place the pea husks in a clean, sealable jar and pour the gin over the top. Cover and let sit for five to seven days. Strain through cheesecloth to remove any debris and store in a clean, sealable jar. Label appropriately.

To prepare the cocktail:

Combine all ingredients in a Collins glass. Fill with ice and top with tonic water. Garnish with fresh sweet peas in the husk and fresh mint.

ALIZA BARAN

Cucumber Mango Shrub

Mindy McCord, Siren Shrub Co.

This refreshing beverage incorporates the tropical notes of mango with refreshing cucumber and the herbal notes of basil and mint. It's a delectable drink that can be enjoyed year-round, but it's particularly amazing on a cold winter day in Wisconsin when one wants nothing more than an escape to a tropical clime. The Basil Siren Shrub used in this drink features basil grown by Whitefeather Organics in Custer, Wisconsin.

MAKES 1 MOCKTAIL

For the mango puree:

1 ripe mango, seed and skin removed, chopped

1 cup water

1 cup sugar

For the mocktail:

1½ ounces mango puree

1 ounce Basil Siren Shrub

2 cucumber wheels

seltzer

mint sprig, for garnish

To prepare the mango puree:

Add mango to a blender jar with water and sugar. Blend until emulsified. This process makes more than you'll need for one drink, but it will keep in the refrigerator for at least two weeks.

To prepare the mocktail:

In a Collins glass, add mango puree, Basil Siren Shrub, and cucumber wheels to the glass. Muddle in the base of the glass until the cucumber is thoroughly broken down. Add ice, and top with seltzer. Give the mixture a quick stir to incorporate and garnish with a mint sprig.

SIREN SHRUB CO.

Thyme Weaver

Corey Ochoa, Saffron
with thyme from Baby Mama Botanicals

Syrup made with Wisconsin maple syrup and locally sourced thyme from Baby Mama Botanicals creates a base for this refreshingly playful take on a whiskey sour from the mixologist at Saffron Modern Indian Dining in Milwaukee.

MAKES 1 COCKTAIL

For the maple thyme syrup:

2 cups water

2 cups light brown sugar

1 cup pure Wisconsin maple syrup

½ ounce thyme leaves

For the drink:

½ ounce fresh lemon juice

½ ounce fresh orange juice

1 ounce maple thyme syrup

1½ ounce Uncle Nearest 1884 whiskey

fresh thyme sprig, for garnish

To prepare the syrup:

Add water, brown sugar, and maple syrup to a medium saucepan. Bring to a simmer over medium heat, stirring occasionally. Once the sugar dissolves and liquid starts to simmer, add thyme and allow the mixture to cook for an additional 5 minutes. Remove from heat, cover, and cool the syrup to room temperature. Once cool, strain out thyme. Store the syrup in an airtight container in the refrigerator. Syrup will keep for up to one month.

To prepare the drink:

Combine all ingredients into a shaker tin and fill with ice. Shake vigorously and double strain into a coupe glass. Garnish with a sprig of fresh thyme before serving.

COREY OCHOA/SAFFRON

The Beet Down

Bartenders at Wickman House
with beets from the Wickman House Garden

The earthy sweetness of beets comes together with the zing of ginger and fresh mint in this refreshing quaff that is as beautiful as it is delicious.

MAKES 1 COCKTAIL

5 local berries (blackberry, blueberry, or strawberry)

5 fresh mint leaves

½ tablespoon sugar

2 ounces London dry gin

1½ ounces fresh beet juice

ginger beer (the spicier, the better)

1 sprig of fresh mint, for garnish

Muddle the berries, mint, and sugar in a cocktail shaker. Add gin and beet juice, along with ice. Shake vigorously to combine. Using a julep strainer and a fine mesh sieve, double strain into a Collins glass, and add fresh ice. Top with ginger beer and garnish with mint sprig.

XOME STUDIO

GRATITUDE

This book is a love letter.

It's an homage to the farmers whose fingers coax life from warm soil.

It's dedicated to the chefs whose imaginations run wild in the kitchen and the cooks who are inspired by their creativity.

It's a snapshot of a moment in time in the food world.

But this book was also a collaboration. I owe much to the farmers who broke away from their chores—even during the peak of the season—and made time for conversations with me about the work they do.

I am grateful to the chefs who—despite the stress and challenges of the COVID-19 pandemic—were willing to share their knowledge and take time to write down their recipes amid staff shortages and emotional and mental exhaustion. For those of you who helped me fill in the gaps at the eleventh hour (you know who you are), I'll be forever grateful. I'm also indebted to Jan Kelly, who generously heeded my request to write about her experiences as a chef and shared an intimate portrait of her life and career in Wisconsin.

I'm appreciative of the photographers who shared their talents to ensure this book would be filled with eye-catching images. And I'd be remiss in not acknowledging the tourism bureaus and public relations professionals who assisted me in rounding out my list of restaurant contacts and pointing me toward new restaurants that hadn't yet made it onto my radar.

Last, but not least, I want to offer many thanks to the people in my life who contributed to yet another one of my crazy writing endeavors.

To Kristine Hansen for helping me land the contract for my book and offering support as only a fellow writer can.

To Stephanie Traska for plying me with wine, spicy gherkins, and muffins and patiently assisting me in standardizing the formatting for recipes.

To my husband, Paul, for leaving me the very last cracker and piece of Gouda as I struggled to finish my manuscript in the final hours before my deadline. You are my Carrot Snack Cake.

To you for supporting my work (and reading this far).

INDEX OF RECIPES AND INGREDIENTS

ABOUT THE AUTHOR

Lori Fredrich is the senior food writer and dining editor for OnMilwaukee. She is also the author of *Milwaukee Food: A History of Cream City Cuisine* and co-host of *FoodCrush*, a podcast "for people who eat."

Lori is an avid cook whose accrual of condiments and spices is rivaled only by her cookbook collection. Her passion for the culinary industry was birthed while balancing A&W root beer mugs as a teenage carhop, fed by insatiable curiosity, and further fueled by the people whose stories entwine with each and every dish.

Over the years, her recipes and writing have been featured in a variety of publications, including *Cheese Connoisseur, Cooking Light, Edible Milwaukee, Milwaukee Magazine,* and *the Milwaukee Journal Sentinel.*

SIMON MCCONICO